The
Greatest Thing
in the World

The Greatest Thing in the World

And 7 Other Addresses

HENRY DRUMMOND

MEDIA

Published 2019 by Gildan Media LLC
aka G&D Media
www.GandDmedia.com

THE GREATEST THING IN THE WORLD. Copyright © 2019 by G&D Media.
All rights reserved. *The Greatest Thing in the World* was originally
published in 1891 and 1898 by Fleming H. Revell Company.

Front cover design by David Rheinhardt of Pyrographx

Interior design by Meghan Day Healey of Story Horse, LLC

Library of Congress Cataloging-in-Publication Data is available
upon request

ISBN: 978-1-7225-0281-2

10 9 8 7 6 5 4 3 2 1

Contents

Introductory

I was staying with a party of friends in a country house during my visit to England in 1884. On Sunday evening as we sat around the fire, they asked me to read and expound some portion of Scripture. Being tired after the services of the day, I told them to ask Henry Drummond, who was one of the party. After some urging he drew a small Testament from his hip pocket, opened it at the 13th chapter of I Corinthians, and began to speak on the subject of Love.

It seemed to me that I had never heard anything so beautiful, and I determined not to rest until I brought Henry Drummond to Northfield to deliver that address. Since then I have requested the principals of my schools to have it read before the students every year. The one great need in our Christian life is love, more love to God and to each other. Would that we could all move into that Love chapter, and live there.

—D.L. Moody

This volume contains, in addition to the address on Love, some other addresses which I trust will bring help and blessing to many.

> *Though I speak with the tongues of men and of angels, and have not love, I am become as sounding brass, or a tinkling cymbal. And though I have the gift of prophecy, and understand all mys teries, and all knowledge; and though I have all faith, so that I could remove mountains, and have not love, I am nothing. And though I bestow all my goods to feed the poor and though I gave my body to be burned, and have not love, it profiteth me nothing.*
> *Love suffereth long, and is kind;*
> *Love envieth not;*
> *Love wanteth not itself, is not puffed up,*
> *Doth no behave itself unseemly,*
> *Seeketh not her own,*

Is not easily provoked,

Thinketh no evil;

Rejoiceth not in iniquity, but rejoiceth in the truth;

Beareth all things, believeth all things, hopeth all things, endureth all things.

Love never faileth: but whether there be prophecies, they shall fail; whether there be tongues, they shall cease; whether there be knowledge, it shall vanish away. For we know in part, and we prophesy in part. But when that which is perfect is come, then that which is in part shall be done away. When I was a child, I spake as a child, I understood as a child, I thought as a child: but when I became a man, I put away childish things. For now we see through a glass, darkly; but then face to face: now I know in part; but then shall I know even as also I am known. And now abideth faith, hope, love, these three; but the greatest of these is love.

—1 Corinthians 13

Love: The Greatest Thing In the World

Every one has asked himself the great question of antiquity as of the modern world: What is the *summum bonum*—the supreme good? You have life before you. Once only you can live it. What is the noblest object of desire, the supreme gift to covet?

We have been accustomed to be told that the greatest thing in the religious world is Faith. That great word has been the key-note for centuries of the popular religion; and we have easily learned to look upon it as the greatest thing in the world. Well, we are wrong. If we have been told that, we may miss the mark. In the 13th chapter of I

Corinthians, Paul takes us to CHRISTIANITY AT ITS SOURCE; and there we see, "The greatest of these is love."

It is not an oversight. Paul was speaking of faith just a moment before. He says, "If I have all faith, so that I can remove mountains, and have not love, I am nothing." So far from forgetting, he deliberately contrasts them, "Now abideth Faith, Hope, Love," and without a moment's hesitation the decision falls, "The greatest of these is Love."

And it is not prejudice. A man is apt to recommend to others his own strong point. Love was not Paul's strong point. The observing student can detect a beautiful tenderness growing and ripening all through his character as Paul gets old; but the hand that wrote, "The greatest of these is love," when we meet it first, is stained with blood.

Nor is this letter to the Corinthians peculiar in singling out love as the *summum bonum*. The masterpieces of Christianity are agreed about it. Peter says, "Above all things have fervent love among yourselves." *Above all things.* And John goes farther, "God is love."

You remember the profound remark which Paul makes elsewhere, "Love is the fulfilling of the law." Did you ever think what he meant by that? In those days men were working the passage to Heaven by keeping the Ten Commandments, and the hundred and ten other commandments which they had manufactured out of them. Christ came and said, "I will show you a more simple way. If you do one thing, you will do these hundred and ten things, without ever thinking about them. If you *love*, you will unconsciously fulfill the whole law."

You can readily see for yourselves how that must be so. Take any of the commandments. "Thou shalt have no other gods before Me." If a man love God, you will not require to tell him that. Love is the fulfilling of that law. "Take not His name in vain." Would he ever dream of taking His name in vain if he loved him? "Remember the Sabbath day to keep it holy." Would he not be too glad to have one day in seven to dedicate more exclusively to the object of his affection? Love would fulfill all these laws regarding God.

And so, if he loved man, you would never think of telling him to honor his father and mother. He could not do anything else. It would be preposterous to tell him not to kill. You could only insult him if you suggested that he should not steal— how could he steal from those he loved? It would be superfluous to beg him not to bear false witness against his neighbor. If he loved him it would be the last thing he would do. And you would never dream of urging him not to covet what his neighbors had. He would rather they possessed it than himself. In this way "Love is the fulfilling of the law." It is the rule for fulfilling all rules, the new commandment for keeping all the old commandments, Christ's one SECRET OF THE CHRISTIAN LIFE. Now Paul has learned that; and in this noble eulogy he has given us the most wonderful and original account extant of the *summum bonum*. We may divide it into three parts. In the beginning of the short chapter we have Love *contrasted*; in the heart of it, we have Love *analyzed*; toward the end, we have Love *defended* as the supreme gift.

I. THE CONTRAST.

Paul begins by contrasting Love with other things that men in those days thought much of. I shall not attempt to go over these things in detail. Their inferiority is already obvious.

He contrasts it with *eloquence*. And what a noble gift it is, the power of playing upon the souls and wills of men, and rousing them to lofty purposes and holy deeds! Paul says, "If I speak with the tongues of men and of angels, and have not love, I am become sounding brass, or a tinkling cymbal." We all know why. We have all felt the brazenness of words without emotion, the hollowness, the unaccountable unpersuasiveness, of eloquence behind which lies no Love.

He contrasts it with *prophecy*. He contrasts it with *mysteries*. He contrasts it with *faith*. He contrasts it with *charity*. Why is Love greater than faith? Because the end is greater than the means. And why is it greater than charity? Because the whole is greater than the part.

Love is greater than *faith*, because the end is greater than the means. What is the use of having faith? It is to connect the soul with God. And what is the object of connecting man with God? That he may become like God. But God is Love. Hence Faith, the means, is in order to Love, the end. Love, therefore, obviously is greater than faith. "If I have all faith, so as to remove mountains, but have not love, I am nothing."

It is greater than *charity*, again, because the whole is greater than a part. Charity is only a little bit of Love, one of the innumerable avenues of Love, and there may even be, and there is, a great deal of charity without Love. It is a very easy thing to toss a copper to a beggar on the street; it is generally an easier thing than not to do it. Yet Love is just as often in the withholding. We purchase relief from the sympathetic feelings roused by the spectacle of misery, at the copper's cost. It is too cheap—too cheap for us, and often too dear for the beggar. If we really loved him we would either do more for him, or less. Hence, "If I bestow all my goods to feed the poor, but have not love it profiteth me nothing."

Then Paul contrasts it with *sacrifice* and martyrdom: "If I give my body to be burned, but have not love, it profiteth me nothing." Missionaries can take nothing greater to the heathen world than the impress and reflection of the Love of God upon their own character. That is the universal language. It will take them years to speak in Chinese, or in the dialects of India. From the day they land, that language of Love, understood by all, will be pouring forth its unconscious eloquence.

It is the man who is the missionary, it is not his words. His character is his message. In the heart of Africa, among the great Lakes, I have come across black men and women who remembered the only white man they ever saw before—David Livingstone; and as you cross his footsteps in that dark continent, MEN'S FACES LIGHT UP as they speak of the kind doctor who passed there years ago. They could not understand him; but they felt the love that beat in his heart. They knew that it was love, although he spoke no word.

Take into your sphere of labor, where you also mean to lay down your life, that simple charm, and your lifework must succeed. You can take nothing greater, you need take nothing less. You may take every accomplishment; you may be braced for every sacrifice; but if you give your body to be burned, and have not Love, it will profit you and the cause of Christ *nothing*.

II. THE ANALYSIS.

After contrasting Love with these things, Paul, in three verses, very short, gives us an amazing analysis of what this supreme thing is.

I ask you to look at it. It is a compound thing, he tells us. It is like light. As you have seen a man of science take a beam of light and pass it through a crystal prism, as you have seen it come out on the other side of the prism broken up into its component colors—red, and blue, and yellow, and violet, and orange, and all the colors of the rainbow—so Paul passes this thing, Love, through the magnificent prism of his inspired intellect, and it comes out on the other side broken up into its elements.

In these few words we have what one might call THE SPECTRUM OF LOVE, the analysis of Love. Will you observe what its elements are? Will you notice that they have common names; that they are virtues which we hear about every day; that they are things which can be practised by every man in every place in life; and how, by a multitude of small things and ordinary virtues, the supreme thing, the *summum bonum*, is made up?

The Spectrum of Love has nine ingredients:

Patience	"Love suffereth long."
Kindness	"And is kind."
Generosity	"Love envieth not."
Humility	"Love vaunteth not itself, is not puffed up."
Courtesy	"Doth not behave itself unseemly."
Unselfishness	"Seeketh not its own."
Good temper	"Is not provoked."
Guilelessness	"Taketh not account of evil."
Sincerity	"Rejoiceth not in unrighteousness, but rejoiceth with the truth."

Patience; *kindness*; *generosity*; *humility*; *courtesy*; *unselfishness*; *good temper*; *guilelessness*; *sincerity*—these make up the supreme gift, the stature of the perfect man.

You will observe that all are in relation to men, in relation to life, in relation to the known to-day and the near to-morrow, and not to the unknown eternity. We hear much of love to God; Christ spoke much of love to man. We make a great deal of peace with heaven; Christ made much of peace on earth. Religion is not a strange or added thing, but the inspiration of the secular life, the breathing of an eternal spirit through this temporal world.

The supreme thing, in short, is not a thing at all, but the giving of a further finish to the multitudinous words and acts which make up the sum of every common day.

Patience. This is the normal attitude of love; Love passive, Love waiting to begin; not in a hurry; calm; ready to do its work when the summons comes, but meantime wearing the ornament of a meek and quiet spirit. Love suffers long; beareth all things; believeth all things; hopeth all things. For Love understands, and therefore waits.

Kindness. Love active. Have you ever noticed how much of Christ's life was spent in doing kind things—in *merely* doing kind things? Run over it with that in view, and you will find that He spent a great proportion of His time simply in making people happy, in DOING GOOD TURNS to people. There is only one thing greater than happiness in the world, and that is holiness; and it is not in our keeping; but what God *has* put in our power is the happiness of those about us, and that is largely to be secured by our being kind to them.

"The greatest thing," says some one, "a man can do for his Heavenly Father is to be kind to some of His other children." I wonder why it is that we are not all kinder than we are? How much the world needs it! How easily it is done! How instantaneously it acts! How infallibly it is remem-

bered! How superabundantly it pays itself back—
for there is no debtor in the world so honorable, so
superbly honorable, as Love. "Love never faileth."
Love is success, Love is happiness, Love is life.
"Love," I say with Browning, "is energy of life."

"For life, with all it yields of joy or woe
And hope and fear,
Is just our chance o' the prize of learning love,—
How love might be, hath been indeed, and is."

Where Love is, God is. He that dwelleth in
Love dwelleth in God. God is Love. Therefore
love. Without distinction, without calculation,
without procrastination, love. Lavish it upon the
poor, where it is very easy; especially upon the
rich, who often need it most; most of all upon our
equals, where it is very difficult, and for whom
perhaps we each do least of all. There is a difference between *trying to please* and *giving pleasure.*
Give pleasure. Lose no chance of giving pleasure;
for that is the ceaseless and anonymous triumph
of a truly loving spirit. "I shall pass through this
world but once. Any good thing, therefore, that
I can do, or any kindness that I can show to any
human being, let me do it now. Let me not defer it
or neglect it, for I shall not pass this way again."

Generosity. "Love envieth not." This is love in competition with others. Whenever you attempt a good work you will find other men doing the same kind of work, and probably doing it better. Envy them not. Envy is a feeling of ill-will to those who are in the same line as ourselves, a spirit of covetousness and detraction. How little Christian work even is a protection against un-Christian feeling! That most despicable of all the unworthy moods which cloud a Christian's soul assuredly waits for us on the threshold of every work, unless we are fortified with this grace of magnanimity. Only one thing truly need the Christian envy—the large, rich, generous soul which "envieth not."

And then, after having learned all that, you have to learn this further thing, *Humility*—to put a seal upon your lips and forget what you have done. After you have been kind, after Love has stolen forth into the world and done its beautiful work, go back into the shade again and say nothing about it. Love hides even from itself. Love waives even self-satisfaction. "Love vaunteth not itself, is not puffed up." Humility—love hiding.

The fifth ingredient is a somewhat strange one to find in this *summum bonum*: *Courtesy*. This is Love in society, Love in relation to etiquette. "Love does not behave itself unseemly."

Politeness has been defined as love in trifles. Courtesy is said to be love in little things. And the one secret of politeness is to love.

Love *cannot* behave itself unseemly. You can put the most untutored persons into the highest society, and if they have a reservoir of Love in their heart they will not behave themselves unseemly. They simply cannot do it. Carlisle said of Robert Burns that there was no truer gentleman in Europe than the ploughman-poet. It was because he loved everything—the mouse, and the daisy, and all the things, great and small, that God had made. So with this simple passport he could mingle with any society, and enter courts and palaces from his little cottage on the banks of the Ayr.

You know the meaning of the word "gentleman." It means a gentle man—a man who does things gently, with love. That is the whole art and mystery of it. The gentle man cannot in the nature of things do an ungentle, an ungentlemanly thing. The ungentle soul, the inconsiderate, unsympathetic nature, cannot do anything else. "Love doth not behave itself unseemly."

Unselfishness. "Love seeketh not her own." Observe: Seeketh not even that which is her own. In Britain the Englishman is devoted, and rightly, to his rights. But there come times when a man may exercise even THE HIGHER RIGHT of giving up his rights.

Yet Paul does not summon us to give up our rights. Love strikes much deeper. It would have us not seek them at all, ignore them, eliminate the personal element altogether from our calculations.

It is not hard to give up our rights. They are often eternal. The difficult thing is to give up *ourselves*. The more difficult thing still is not to seek things for ourselves at all. After we have sought them, bought them, won them, deserved them, we have taken the cream off them for ourselves already. Little cross then to give them up. But not to seek them, to look every man not on his own things, but on the things of others—that is the difficulty. "Seekest thou great things for thyself?" said the prophet; "*seek them not.*" Why? Because there is no greatness in *things*. Things cannot be great. The only greatness is unselfish love. Even self-denial in itself is nothing, is almost a mistake. Only a great purpose or a mightier love can justify the waste.

It is more difficult, I have said, not to seek our own at all than, having sought it, to give it up. I must take that back. It is only true of a partly selfish heart. Nothing is a hardship to Love, and nothing is hard. I believe that Christ's "yoke" is easy. Christ's yoke is just His way of taking life.

And I believe it is an easier way than any other. I believe it is a happier way than any other. The most obvious lesson in Christ's teaching is that there is no happiness in having and getting anything, but only in giving. I repeat, *there is no happiness in having or in getting, but only in giving.* Half the world is on the wrong scent in pursuit of happiness. They think it consists in having and getting, and in being served by others. It consists in giving, and in serving others. "He that would be great among you," said Christ, "let him serve." He that would be happy, let him remember that there is but one way—"it is more blessed, it is more happy, to give than to receive."

The next ingredient is a very remarkable one: *Good temper.* "Love is not provoked."

Nothing could be more striking than to find this here. We are inclined to look upon bad temper as a very harmless weakness. We speak of it as a mere infirmity of nature, a family failing, a matter of temperament, not a thing to take into very serious account in estimating a man's character. And yet here, right in the heart of this analysis of love, it finds a place; and the Bible again and again returns to condemn it as one of the most destructive elements in human nature.

The peculiarity of ill temper is that it is the vice of the virtuous. It is often the one blot on an otherwise noble character. You know men who are all but perfect, and women who would be entirely perfect, but for an easily ruffled, quick-tempered, or "touchy" disposition. This compatibility of ill temper with high moral character is one of the strangest and saddest problems of ethics. The truth is, there are two great classes of sins—sins of the *Body* and sins of the *Disposition*. The Prodigal Son may be taken as a type of the first, the Elder Brother of the second. Now, society has no doubt whatever as to which of these is the worse. Its brand falls, without a challenge, upon the Prodigal. But are we right? We have no balance to weigh one another's sins, and coarser and finer are but human words; but faults in the higher nature may be less venal than those in the lower, and to the eye of Him who is Love, a sin against Love may seem a hundred times more base. No form of vice, not worldliness, not greed of gold, not drunkenness itself, does more to un-Christianize society than evil temper. For embittering life, for breaking up communities, for destroying the most sacred relationships, for devastating homes, for withering up men and women, for taking the bloom of childhood, in short, FOR SHEER GRATUITOUS MISERY-PRODUCING POWER this influence stands alone.

Look at the Elder Brother—moral, hard-working, patient, dutiful—let him get all credit for his virtues—look at this man, this baby, sulking outside his own father's door. "He was angry," we read, "and would not go in." Look at the effect upon the father, upon the servants, upon the happiness of the guests. Judge of the effect upon the Prodigal—and how many prodigals are kept out of the Kingdom of God by the unlovely character of those who profess to be inside. Analyze, as a study in Temper, the thunder-cloud itself as it gathers upon the Elder Brother's brow. What is it made of? Jealousy, anger, pride, uncharity, cruelty, self-righteousness, touchiness, doggedness, sullenness—these are the ingredients of this dark and loveless soul. In varying proportions, also, these are the ingredients of all ill temper. Judge if such sins of the disposition are not worse to live in, and for others to live with, than the sins of the body. Did Christ indeed not answer the question Himself when He said, "I say unto you that the publicans and the harlots go into the Kingdom of Heaven before you"? There is really no place in heaven for a disposition like this. A man with such a mood could only make heaven miserable for all the people in it. Except, therefore, such a man be BORN AGAIN, he cannot, simply *cannot*, enter the kingdom of heaven.

You will see then why Temper is significant. It is not in what it is alone, but in what it reveals.

This is why I speak of it with such unusual plain-ness. It is a test for love, a symptom, a revelation of an unloving nature at bottom. It is the intermit-tent fever which bespeaks unintermittent disease within; the occasional bubble escaping to the sur-face which betrays some rottenness underneath; a sample of the most hidden products of the soul dropped involuntarily when off one's guard; in a word, the lightning form of a hundred hideous and un-Christian sins. A want of patience, a want of kindness, a want of generosity, a want of courtesy, a want of unselfishness, are all instantaneously symbolized in one flash of Temper.

Hence it is not enough to deal with the Tem-per. We must go to the source, and change the inmost nature, and the angry humors will die away of themselves. Souls are made sweet not by tak-ing the acid fluids out, but by putting something in—a great Love, a new Spirit, the Spirit of Christ. Christ, the Spirit of Christ, interpenetrating ours, sweetens, purifies, transforms all. This only can eradicate what is wrong, work a chemical change, renovate and regenerate, and rehabilitate the inner man. Will-power does not change men. Time does not change men. CHRIST DOES. Therefore, "Let that mind be in you which was also in Christ Jesus."

Some of us have not much time to lose. Remem-ber, once more, that this is a matter of life or death.

I cannot help speaking urgently, for myself, for yourselves. "Whoso shall offend one of these little ones, which believe in me, it were better for him that a millstone were hanged about his neck, and that he were drowned in the depth of the sea." That is to say, it is the deliberate verdict of the Lord Jesus that it is better not to live than not to love. *It is better not to live than not to love.*

Guilelessness and *Sincerity* may be dismissed almost without a word. Guilelessness is the grace for suspicious people. The possession of it is THE GREAT SECRET OF PERSONAL INFLUENCE. You will find, if you think for a moment, that the people who influence you are people who believe in you. In an atmosphere of suspicion men shrivel up; but in that atmosphere they expand, and find encouragement and educative fellowship.

It is a wonderful thing that here and there in this hard, uncharitable world there should still be left a few rare souls who think no evil. This is the great unworldliness. Love "thinketh no evil," imputes no motive, sees the bright side, puts the best construction on every action. What a delightful state of mind to live in! What a stimulus and benediction even to meet with it for a day! To be trusted is to be saved. And if we try to influence or elevate others, we shall soon see that success is in proportion to their belief of our belief in them.

The respect of another is the first restoration of the self-respect a man has lost; our ideal of what he is becomes to him the hope and pattern of what he may become.

"Love rejoiceth not in unrighteousness, but rejoiceth with the truth." I have called this *Sincerity* from the words rendered in the Authorized Version by "rejoiceth in the truth." And, certainly, were this the real translation, nothing could be more just; for he who loves will love Truth not less than men. He will rejoice in the Truth—rejoice not in what he has been taught to believe; not in this church's doctrine or in that; not in this ism or in that ism; but "in *the Truth*." He will accept only what is real; he will strive to get at facts; he will search for *Truth* with a humble and unbiased mind, and cherish whatever he finds at any sacrifice. But the more literal translation of the Revised Version calls for just such a sacrifice for truth's sake here. For what Paul really meant is, as we there read, "Rejoiceth not in unrighteousness, but rejoiceth with the truth," a quality which probably no one English word—and certainly not *Sincerity*—adequately defines. It includes, perhaps more strictly, the self-restraint which refuses to make capital out of others' faults; the charity which delights not in exposing the weakness of others, but "covereth all things"; the sincerity of purpose which endeavors to see things as they are, and rejoices to find them better than suspicion feared or calumny denounced.

So much for the analysis of Love. Now the business of our lives is to have these things fitted into our characters. That is the supreme work to which we need to address ourselves in this world, to learn Love. Is life not full of opportunities for learning Love? Every man and woman every day has a thousand of them. The world is not a playground; it is a schoolroom. Life is not a holiday, but an education. And THE ONE ETERNAL LESSON for us all is *how better we can love.*

What makes a man a good cricketer? Practice. What makes a man a good artist, a good sculptor, a good musician? Practice. What makes a man a good linguist, a good stenographer? Practice. What makes a man a good man? Practice. Nothing else. There is nothing capricious about religion. We do not get the soul in different ways, under different laws, from those in which we get the body and the mind. If a man does not exercise his arm he develops no biceps muscle; and if a man does not exercise his soul, he acquires no muscle in his soul, no strength of character, no vigor of moral fibre, no beauty of spiritual growth. Love is not a thing of enthusiastic emotion. It is a rich, strong, manly, vigorous expression of the whole round Christian character—the Christlike nature in its fullest development. And the constituents of this great character are only to be built up by CEASELESS PRACTICE.

What was Christ doing in the carpenter's shop? Practising. Though perfect, we read that He *learned* obedience, and grew in wisdom and in favor with God. Do not quarrel, therefore, with your lot in life. Do not complain of its never-ceasing cares, its petty environment, the vexations you have to stand, the small and sordid souls you have to live and work with. Above all, do not resent temptation; do not be perplexed because it seems to thicken round you more and more, and ceases neither for effort nor for agony nor prayer. That is your practice. That is the practice which God appoints you; and it is having its work in making you patient, and humble, and generous, and unselfish, and kind, and courteous. Do not grudge the hand that is moulding the still too shapeless image within you. It is growing more beautiful, though you see it not; and every touch of temptation may add to its perfection. Therefore keep in the midst of life. Do not isolate yourself. Be among men and among things, and among troubles, and difficulties, and obstacles. You remember Goethe's words: "Talent develops itself in solitude; character in the stream of life." Talent develops itself in

solitude—the talent of prayer, of faith, of meditation, of seeing the unseen; character grows in the
stream of the world's life. That chiefly is where
men are to learn love.

How? Now, how? To make it easier, I have
named a few of the elements of love. But these
are only elements. Love itself can never be
defined. Light is a something more than the sum
of its ingredients—a glowing, dazzling, tremu-
lous ether. And love is something more than all
its elements—a palpitating, quivering, sensitive,
living thing. By synthesis of all the colors, men
can make whiteness, they cannot make light. By
synthesis of all the virtues, men can make virtue,
they cannot make love. How then are we to have
this transcendent living whole conveyed into our
souls? We brace our wills to secure it. We try to
copy those who have it. We lay down rules about
it. We watch. We pray. But these things alone will
not bring love into our nature. Love is an *effect*.
And only as we fulfill the right condition can we
have the effect produced. Shall I tell you what the
cause is?

If you turn to the Revised Version of the First
Epistle of John you find these words: "We love
because He first loved us." "We love," not "We love
Him." That is the way the old version has it, and it
is quite wrong. "*We love*—because He first loved

us." Look at that word "because." It is the *cause* of which I have spoken. "*Because* He first loved us," the effect follows that we love, we love Him, we love all men. We cannot help it. Because He loved us, we love, we love everybody. Our heart is slowly changed. Contemplate the love of Christ, and you will love. Stand before that mirror, reflect Christ's character, and you will be changed into the same image from tenderness to tenderness. There is no other way. You cannot love to order. You can only look at the lovely object, and fall in love with it, and grow into likeness to it. And so look at this Perfect Character, this Perfect Life. Look at THE GREAT SACRIFICE as He laid down Himself, all through life, and upon the Cross of Calvary; and you must love Him. And loving Him, you must become like Him. Love begets love. It is a process of induction. Put a piece of iron in the presence of an electrified body, and that piece of iron for a time becomes electrified. It is changed into a temporary magnet in the mere presence of a permanent magnet, and as long as you leave the two side by side, they are both magnets alike. Remain side by side with Him who loved us, and GAVE HIMSELF FOR US, and you, too, will become a permanent magnet, a permanently attractive force; and like Him you will draw all men unto you, like Him you will be drawn unto all men. That is the inevitable effect of

Love. Any man who fulfills that cause must have that effect produced in him.

Try to give up the idea that religion comes to us by chance, or by mystery, or by caprice. It comes to us by natural law, or by supernatural law, for all law is Divine.

Edward Irving went to see a dying boy once, and when he entered the room he just put his hand on the sufferer's head, and said, "My boy, God loves you," and went away. The boy started from his bed, and called out to the people in the house, "God loves me! God loves me!" One word! It changed that boy. The sense that God loved him overpowered him, melted him down, and began the creating of a new heart in him. And that is how the love of God melts down the unlovely heart in man, and begets in him the new creature, who is patient and humble and gentle and unselfish. And there is no other way to get it. There is no mystery about it. We love others, we love everybody, we love our enemies, *because He first loved us.*

III. THE DEFENCE.

Now I have a closing sentence or two to add about Paul's reason for singling out love as the supreme possession.

It is a very remarkable reason. In a single word it is this: *it lasts.* "Love," urges Paul, "never faileth." Then he begins again one of his marvelous lists of the great things of the day, and exposes them one by one. He runs over the things that men thought were going to last, and shows that they are all fleeting, temporary, passing away.

"Whether there be *prophecies*, they shall be done away." It was the mother's ambition for her boy in those days that he should become a prophet. For hundreds of years God had never spoken by means of any prophet, and at that time the prophet was greater than the king. Men waited wistfully for another messenger to come, and hung upon his lips when he appeared, as upon the very voice of God. Paul says, "Whether there be prophecies, they shall fail." The Bible is full of prophecies. One by one they have "failed"; that is, having been fulfilled, their work is finished; they have nothing more to do now in the world except to feed a devout man's faith.

Then Paul talks about *tongues.* That was another thing that was greatly coveted. "Whether there be tongues, they shall cease." As we all know, many many centuries have passed since tongues have been known in this world. They have ceased. Take it in any sense you like. Take it, for illustration merely, as languages in general—a sense which was not in Paul's mind at all, and which though it cannot give us the specific lesson, will point the general truth. Consider the words in which these chapters were written—Greek. It has gone. Take the Latin—the other great tongue of those days. It ceased long ago. Look at the Indian language. It is ceasing. The language of Wales, of Ireland, of the Scottish Highlands is dying before our eyes. The most popular book in the English tongue at the present time, except the Bible, is one of Dickens' works, his *Pickwick Papers*. It is largely written in the language of London street-life; and experts assure us that in fifty years it will be unintelligible to the average English reader.

Then Paul goes farther, and with even greater boldness adds, "Whether there be *knowledge*, it shall be done away." The wisdom of the ancients, where is it? It is wholly gone. A schoolboy to-day knows more than Sir Isaac Newton knew; his knowledge has vanished away. You put yesterday's newspaper in the fire: its knowledge has vanished away. You buy the old editions of the great encyclopædias for a few cents: their knowledge has vanished away. Look how the coach has been superseded by the use of steam. Look how electricity has superseded that, and swept a hundred almost new inventions into oblivion. One of the greatest living authorities, Sir William Thompson, said in Scotland, at a meeting at which I was present, "The steam-engine is passing away." "Whether there be knowledge, it shall vanish away." At every workshop you will see, in the back yard, a heap of old iron, a few wheels, a few levers, a few cranks, broken and eaten with rust. Twenty years ago that was the pride of the city. Men flocked in from the country to see the great invention; now it is superseded, its day is done. And all the boasted science and philosophy of this day will soon be old.

In my time, in the university of Edinburgh, the greatest figure in the faculty was Sir James Simpson, the discoverer of chloroform. Recently his successor and nephew, Professor Simpson, was asked by the librarian of the University to go to the library and pick out the books on his subject (midwifery) that were no longer needed. His reply to the librarian was this:

"Take every text-book that is more than ten years old and put it down in the cellar."

Sir James Simpson was a great authority only a few years ago: men came from all parts of the earth to consult him; and almost the whole teaching of that time is consigned by the science of to-day to oblivion. And in every branch of science it is the same. "Now we know in part. We see through a glass darkly." Knowledge does not last.

Can you tell me anything that is going to last? Many things Paul did not condescend to name. He did not mention money, fortune, fame; but he picked out the great things of his time, the things the best men thought had something in them, and brushed them peremptorily aside. Paul had no charge against these things in themselves. All he said about them was that they would not last. They were great things, but not supreme things. There were things beyond them. What we are stretches past what we do, beyond what we possess. Many things that men denounce as sins are not sins; but they are temporary. And that is a favorite argument of the New Testament. John says of the world, not that it is wrong, but simply that it "passeth away." There is a great deal in the world that is delightful and beautiful; there is a great deal in it that is great and engrossing; but IT WILL NOT LAST.

All that is in the world, the lust of the eye, the lust of the flesh, and the pride of life, are but for a little while. Love not the world therefore. Nothing that it contains is worth the life and consecration of an immortal soul. The immortal soul must give itself to something that is immortal. And the only immortal things are these: "Now abideth faith, hope, love, but the greatest of these is love."

Some think the time may come when two of these three things will also pass away—faith into sight, hope into fruition. Paul does not say so. We know but little now about the conditions of the life that is to come. But what is certain is that Love must last. God, the Eternal God, is Love. Covet, therefore, that everlasting gift, that one thing which it is certain is going to stand, that one coinage which will be current in the Universe when all the other coinages of all the nations of the world shall be useless and unhonored. You will give yourselves to many things, give yourself first to Love. Hold things in their proportion. *Hold things in their proportion.* Let at least the first great object of our lives be to achieve the character defended in these words, the character—and it is the character of Christ—which is built round Love.

I have said this thing is eternal. Did you ever notice how continually John associates love and faith with eternal life? I was not told when I was a boy that "God so loved the world that He gave His only-begotten Son, that whosoever believeth in Him should have everlasting life." What I was told, I remember, was, that God so loved the world that, if I trusted in Him, I was to have a thing called peace, or I was to have rest, or I was to have joy, or I was to have safety. But I had to find out for myself that whosoever trusteth in Him— that is, whosoever loveth Him, for trust is only the avenue to Love—hath EVERLASTING LIFE.

The Gospel offers a man a life. Never offer a man a thimbleful of Gospel. Do not offer them merely joy, or merely peace, or merely rest, or merely safety; tell them how Christ came to give men a more abundant life than they have, a life abundant in love, and therefore abundant in salvation for themselves, and large in enterprise for the alleviation and redemption of the world. Then only can the Gospel take hold of the whole of a man, body, soul and spirit, and give to each part of his nature its exercise and reward. Many of the current Gospels are addressed only to a part of man's nature. They offer peace, not life; faith, not Love; justification, not regeneration. And men slip back again from such religion because it has never really held them. Their nature was not all in it. It offered no deeper and gladder life-current than the life that was lived before. Surely it stands to reason that only a fuller love can compete with the love of the world.

To love abundantly is to live abundantly, and to love forever is to live forever. Hence, eternal life is inextricably bound up with love. We want to live forever for the same reason that we want to live to-morrow. Why do we want to live to-morrow? Is it because there is some one who loves you, and whom you want to see to-morrow, and be with, and love back? There is no other reason why we should live on than that we love and are beloved. It is when a man has no one to love him that he commits suicide. So long as he has friends, those who love him and whom he loves, he will live, because to live is to love. Be it but the love of a dog, it will keep him in life; but let that go, he has no contact with life, no reason to live. He dies by his own hand.

Eternal life also is to know God, and God is love. This is Christ's own definition. Ponder it. "This is life eternal, that they might know Thee the only true God, and Jesus Christ whom Thou hast sent." Love must be eternal. It is what God is. On the last analysis, then, love is life. Love never faileth, and life never faileth, so long as there is love. That is the philosophy of what Paul is show-ing us; the reason why in the nature of things Love should be the supreme thing—because it is going to last; because in the nature of things it is an Eternal Life. It is a thing that we are living now, not that we get when we die; that we shall have a poor chance of getting when we die unless we are living now. NO WORSE FATE can befall a man in this world than to live and grow old alone, unloving and unloved. To be lost is to live in an unregenerate condition, loveless and unloved; and to be saved is to love; and he that dwelleth in love dwelleth already in God. For God is Love.

Now I have all but finished. How many of you will join me in reading this chapter once a week for the next three months? A man did that once and it changed his whole life. Will you do it? It is for the greatest thing in the world. You might begin by reading it every day, especially the verses which describe the perfect character. "Love suffereth long, and is kind; love envieth not; love vaunteth not itself." Get these ingredients into your life. Then everything that you do is eternal. It is worth doing. It is worth giving time to. No man can become a saint in his sleep; and to fulfill the condition required demands a certain amount of prayer and meditation and time, just as improvement in any direction, bodily or mental, requires preparation and care. Address yourselves to that one thing; at any cost have this transcendent character exchanged for yours.

You will find as you look back upon your life that the moments that stand out, the moments when you have really lived, are the moments when you have done things in a spirit of love. As memory scans the past, above and beyond all the transitory pleasures of life, there leap forward those supreme hours when you have been enabled to do unnoticed kindnesses to those round about you, things too trifling to speak about, but which you feel have entered into your eternal life. I have seen almost all the beautiful things God has made; I have enjoyed almost every pleasure that He has planned for man; and yet as I look back I see standing out above all the life that has gone four or five short experiences, when the love of God reflected itself in some poor imitation, some small act of love of mine, and these seem to be the things which alone of all one's life abide. Everything else in all our lives is transitory. Every other good is visionary. But the acts of love which no man knows about, or can ever know about—they never fail.

In the Book of Matthew, where the Judgment Day is depicted for us in the imagery of One seated upon a throne and dividing the sheep from the goats, the test of a man then is not, "How have I believed?" but "How have I loved?" The test of religion, the final test of religion, is not religiousness, but Love. I say the final test of religion at that great Day is not religiousness, but Love; not what I have done, not what I have believed, not what I have achieved, but how I have discharged the common charities of life. Sins of commission in that awful indictment are not even referred to. By what we have not done, *by sins of omission*, we are judged. It could not be otherwise. For the withholding of love is the negation of the spirit of Christ, the proof that we never knew Him, that for us He lived in vain. It means that He suggested nothing in all our thoughts, that He inspired nothing in all our lives, that we were not once near enough to Him, to be seized with the spell of His compassion for the world. It means that—

> *"I lived for myself, I thought for myself,*
> *For myself, and none beside—*
> *Just as if Jesus had never lived,*
> *As if He had never died."*

Thank God the Christianity of today is coming nearer the world's need. Live to help that on. Thank God men know better, by a hair's breadth, what religion is, what God is, who Christ is, where Christ is. Who is Christ? He who fed the hungry, clothed the naked, visited the sick. And where is Christ? Where?—"Whoso shall receive a little child in My name receiveth Me." And who are Christ's? "Every one that loveth is born of God."

Lessons from
the Angelus

God often speaks to men's souls through music; He also speaks to us through art. Millet's famous painting entitled "The Angelus" is an illuminated text, upon which I am going to say a few words to you to-night.

There are three things in this picture—a potato field, a country lad and a country girl standing in the middle of it, and on the far horizon the spire of a village church. That is all there is to it—no great scenery and no picturesque people. In Roman Catholic countries at the evening hour the church bell rings out to remind the people to pray. Some go into the church, while those that are in the fields bow their heads for a few moments in silent prayer.

That picture contains the three great elements which go to make up a perfectly rounded Christian life. It is not enough to have the "root of the matter" in us, but that we must be whole and entire, lacking nothing. The Angelus may bring to us suggestions as to what constitutes a complete life.

I.

The first element in a symmetrical life is *work*.

Three-fourths of our time is probably spent in work. Of course the meaning of it is that our work should be just as religious as our worship, and unless we can work for the glory of God three-fourths of life remains unsanctified.

The proof that work is religious is that most of Christ's life was spent in work. During a large part of the first thirty years of His life He worked with the hammer and the plane, making ploughs and yokes and household furniture. Christ's public ministry occupied only about two and a half years of His earthly life; the great bulk of His time was simply spent in doing common everyday tasks, and ever since then work has had a new meaning.

When Christ came into the world He was revealed to three deputations who went to meet and worship Him. First came the shepherds, or working class; second, the wise men, or student class; and third, the two old people in the temple, Simeon and Anna; that is to say, Christ is revealed to men at their work, He is revealed to men at their books, and He is revealed to men at their worship. It was the old people who found Christ at their worship, and as we grow older we will spend more time exclusively in worship than we are able to do now. In the mean time we must combine our worship with our work, and we may expect to find Christ at our books and in our common task.

Why should God have provided that so many hours of every day should be occupied with work? It is because WORK MAKES MEN.

A university is not merely a place for making scholars, it is a place for making Christians. A farm is not a place for growing corn, it is a place for growing character, and a man has no character except that which is developed by his life and thought. God's Spirit does the building through the acts which a man performs from day to day. A student who cons out every word in his Latin and Greek instead of consulting a translation finds that honesty is translated into his character. If he works out his mathematical problems thoroughly, he not only becomes a mathematician, but becomes a thorough man. It is by constant and conscientious attention

to daily duties that thoroughness and conscientiousness and honorableness are imbedded in our beings.
Character is THE MUSIC OF THE SOUL, and is
developed by exercise. Active use of the power
entrusted to us is one of the chief means which God
employs for producing the Christian graces. Hence
the religion of a student demands that he be true to
his work, and that he let his Christianity be shown
to his fellow students and to his professors by the
integrity and the conscientiousness of his academic
life. A man who is not faithful in that which is least
will not be faithful in that which is great. I have
known men who struggled unsuccessfully for years
to pass their examinations who, when they became
Christians, found a new motive for work and thus
were able to succeed where previously they had
failed. A man's Christianity comes out as much in
his work as in his worship.

Our work is not only to be done thoroughly,
but it is to be done honestly. A man is not only to
be honorable in his academic relations, but he must
be honest with himself and in his attitude toward
the truth. Students are not entitled to dodge difficulties, they must go down to the foundation principles. Perhaps the truths which are dear to us go
down deeper even than we think, and we will get
more out of them if we dig down for the nuggets
than we will if we only pick up those that are on

the surface. Other theories may perhaps be found to have false bases; if so, we ought to know it. It is well to take our soundings in every direction to see if there is deep water; if there are shoals we ought to find out where they are. Therefore, when we come to difficulties, let us not jump lightly over them, but let us be honest as seekers after truth.

It may not be necessary for people in general to sift the doctrines of Christianity for themselves, but a student is a man whose business it is to think, to exercise the intellect which God has given him in finding out the truth. Faith is never opposed to reason, though it is sometimes supposed by Bible teachers that it is; but you will find it is not. Faith is opposed to sight, but not to reason, though it is not limited to reason. In employing his intellect in the search for truth a student is drawing nearer to the Christ who said, "I am the way, the truth and the life." We talk a great deal about Christ as the way and Christ as the life, but there is a side of Christ especially for the student: "I am the truth," and every student ought to be a truth-lover and a truth-seeker for Christ's sake.

II.

Another element in life, which of course is first in importance, is *God*.

The Angelus is perhaps the most religious picture painted this century. You cannot look at it and see that young man standing in the field with his hat off, and the girl opposite him with her hands clasped and her head bowed on her breast, without feeling a sense of God.

Do we carry about with us the thought of God wherever we go? If not, we have missed the greatest part of life. Do we have a conviction of God's abiding presence wherever we are? There is nothing more needed in this generation than a larger and more Scriptural idea of God. A great American writer has told us that when he was a boy the conception of God which he got from books and sermons was that of a wise and very strict lawyer. I remember well the awful conception of God which I had when a boy. I was given an illustrated edition of Watts' hymns, in which God was represented as a great piercing eye in the midst of a great black thunder cloud. The idea which that picture gave to my young imagination was that of God as a great detective, playing the spy upon my actions, as the hymn says: "Writing now the story of what little children do."

That was a very mistaken and harmful idea which it has taken me years to obliterate. We think of God as "up there," or as one who made the world six thousand years ago and then retired.

We must learn that He is not confined either to time or space. God is not to be thought of as merely back there in time, or up there in space. If not, where is He? "The word is nigh thee, even in thy mouth." The Kingdom of God is within you, and God Himself is among men. When are we to exchange the terrible, far-away, absentee God of our childhood for the everywhere present God of the Bible? Too many of the old Christian writers seem to have conceived of God as not much more than the greatest man—a kind of divine emperor. He is infinitely more; He is a spirit, as Jesus said to the woman at the well, and in Him we live and move and have our being. Let us think of God as Immanuel—God with us—an ever-present, omni-present, eternal One. Long, long ago, God made matter, then He made the flowers and trees and animals, then He made man. Did He stop? Is God dead? If He lives and acts what is He doing? He is MAKING MEN BETTER. He it is that "worketh in you." The buds of our nature are not all out yet; the sap to make them comes from the God who made us, from the indwelling Christ. Our bodies are the temples of the Holy Ghost, and we must bear this in mind, because the sense of God is kept up, not by logic, but by experience.

Until she was seven years of age the life of Helen Keller, the Boston girl who was deaf and dumb and blind, was an absolute blank; nothing could go into that mind because the ears and eyes were closed to the outer world. Then by that great process which has been discovered, by which the blind see, and the deaf hear, and the mute speak, that girl's soul became opened, and they began to put in little bits of knowledge, and bit by bit they began to educate her. They reserved her religious instruction for Phillips Brooks. After some years, when she was twelve years old, they took her to him and he began to talk to her through the young lady who had been the means of opening her senses, and who could communicate with her by the exceedingly delicate process of touch. He began to tell her about God and what He had done, and how He loved men, and what He is to us. The child listened very intelligently, and finally said:

"Mr. Brooks, I knew all that before, but I didn't know His name."

How often we have felt something within us impelling us to do something which we would not have conceived of by ourselves, or enabling us to do something which we could not have done alone. "It is God which worketh in you." This great simple fact EXPLAINS MANY OF THE MYSTERIES OF LIFE, and takes away the fear which we would otherwise have in meeting the difficulties which lie before us.

Two Americans who were crossing the Atlantic met on Sunday night to sing hymns in the cabin. As they sang the hymn, "Jesus, Lover of my Soul," one of the Americans heard an exceedingly rich and beautiful voice behind him. He looked around, and although he did not know the face he thought that he recognized the voice. So when the music ceased he turned around and asked the man if he had not been in the Civil war. The man replied that he had been a Confederate soldier. "Were you at such a place on such a night?" asked the first. "Yes," he said, "and a curious thing happened that night; this hymn recalled it to my mind. I was on sentry duty on the edge of a wood. It was a dark night and very cold, and I was a little frightened because the enemy were supposed to be very near at hand. I felt very homesick and miserable, and about midnight, when everything was very still, I was beginning to feel very weary and thought that I would comfort myself by praying and singing a hymn. I remember singing this hymn,

'All my trust on Thee is stayed,
All my help from Thee I bring,
Cover my defenceless head
With the shadow of Thy wing.'

After I had sung those words a strange peace came down upon me, and through the long night I remember having felt no more fear."

"Now," said the other man, "listen to my story. I was a Union soldier, and was in the wood that night with a party of scouts. I saw you standing up, although I didn't see your face, and my men had their rifles focused upon you waiting the word to fire, but when you sang out,

'Cover my defenceless head
With the shadow of Thy wing,'

I said, 'Boys, put down your rifles, we will go home.' I couldn't kill you after that."

God was working in each of them, in His own way carrying out His will. God keeps his people and guides them and without Him life is but a living death.

III.

The third element in life about which I wish to speak is *love*.

In this picture we notice the delicate sense of companionship, brought out by the young man and the young woman. It matters not whether they are brother and sister, or lover and loved; there have the idea of friendship, the final ingredient in our life, after the two I have named. If the man or the woman had been standing in that field alone it would have been incomplete.

Love is the divine element in life, because "God is love." "He that loveth is born of God," therefore, as some one has said, let us "keep our friendships in repair." Let us cultivate the spirit of friendship, and let the love of Christ develop it into a great love, not only for our friends, but for all humanity. Wherever you go and whatever you do, your work will be a failure unless you have this element in your life.

These three things go far toward forming a well-rounded life. Some of us may not have these ingredients in their right proportion, but if you are lacking in one or the other of them, then pray for it and work for it that your life may be rounded and complete as God intended it should be.

Pax Vobiscum*

I once heard a sermon by a distinguished preacher upon "Rest." It was full of beautiful thoughts; but when I came to ask myself, "How does he say I can get Rest?" there was no answer. The sermon was sincerely meant to be practical, yet it contained no experience that seemed to me to be tangible, nor any advice that I could grasp—any advice, that is to say, which could help me to find the thing itself as I went about the world.

Yet this omission of what is, after all, the only important problem, was not the fault of the preacher. The whole popular religion is in the twi-

---

light here. And when pressed for really working specifics for the experiences with which it deals, it falters, and seems to lose itself in mist.

The want of connection between the great words of religion and every-day life has bewildered and discouraged all of us. Christianity possesses the noblest words in the language; its literature overflows with terms expressive of the greatest and happiest moods which can fill the soul of man. Rest, Joy, Peace, Faith, Love, Light—these words occur with such persistency in hymns and prayers that an observer might think they formed the staple of Christian experience. But on coming to close quarters with the actual life of most of us, how surely would he be disenchanted. I do not think we ourselves are aware how much our religious life is MADE UP OF PHRASES; how much of what we call Christian Experience is only a dialect of the Churches, a mere religious phraseology with almost nothing behind it in what we really feel and know.

To some of us, indeed, the Christian experiences seem further away than when we took the first steps in the Christian life. That life has not opened out as we had hoped. We do not regret our religion, but we are disappointed with it. There are times, perhaps, when wandering notes from a diviner music stray into our spirits; but these experiences come at few and fitful moments. We have no sense of possession in them. When they visit us, it is a surprise. When they leave us, it is without explanation. When we wish their return, we do not know how to secure it.

All which means a religion without solid base, and a poor and flickering life. It means a great bankruptcy in those experiences which give Christianity its personal solace and make it attractive to the world, and a great uncertainty as to any remedy. It is as if we knew everything about health—except the way to get it.

I am quite sure that the difficulty does not lie in the fact that men are not in earnest. This is simply not the fact. All around us Christians are wearing themselves out in trying to be better. The amount of spiritual longing in the world—in the hearts of unnumbered thousands of men and women in whom we should never suspect it; among the wise and thoughtful, among the young and gay, who seldom assuage and never betray their thirst—this is one of the most wonderful and touching facts of life. It is not more heat that is needed, but more light; not more force, but a wiser direction to be given to very real energies already there.

The usual advice when one asks for counsel on these questions is, "Pray." But this advice is far from adequate. I shall qualify the statement presently; but let me urge it here, with what you will perhaps call daring emphasis, that to pray for these things is not the way to get them. No one will get them without praying; but that men do not get them by praying is the simple fact. We have all prayed, and sincerely prayed, for such experiences as I have named; prayed, believing that that was the way to get them. And yet have we got them? The test is experience. I dare not limit prayer; still less the grace of God. If you have got them in this way, it is well. I am speaking to those, be they few or many, who have not got them; to ordinary men in ordinary circumstances. But if we have not got them, it by no means follows that prayer is useless. The correct conclusion is only that it is useless, or inadequate rather, for this particular purpose. To make prayer the sole resort, the universal panacea for every spiritual ill, is as radical a mistake as to prescribe only one medicine for every bodily trouble. The physician who does the last is a quack; the spiritual adviser who does the first is GROSSLY IGNORANT OF HIS PROFESSION. To do nothing but pray is a wrong done to prayer itself, and can only end in disaster. It is as if one tried to live only with the lungs, as if one assimilated only air and neglected solid food. The lungs are a first essential; the air is a first essential; but the body has many members, given for different purposes, secreting different things, and each has a method of nutrition as special to itself as its own activity. While prayer, then, is the characteristic sublimity of the Christian life, it is by no means the only one. And those who make it the sole alternative, and apply it to purposes for which it was never meant, are really doing the greatest harm to prayer itself. To couple the word "inadequate" with this mighty word is not to dethrone prayer, but to exalt it. WHAT DETHRONES PRAYER is unanswered prayer. When men pray for things which do not come that way—pray with sincere belief that prayer, unaided and alone, will compass what they ask—then, not getting what they ask, they often give up prayer.

This is the natural history of much atheism, not only an atheism of atheists, but a more terrible atheism of Christians, an unconscious atheism, whose roots have struck far into many souls whose last breath would be spent in denying it. So, I repeat, it is a mistaken Christianity which allow men to cherish a blind belief in the omnipotence of prayer. Prayer, certainly, when the appropriate conditions are fulfilled, is omnipotent, but not blind prayer. Blind prayer is a superstition. Prayer, in its true sense, contains the sane recognition that while man prays in faith, *God acts by law.* What that means in the immediate connection we shall see presently.

What, then, is the remedy? It is impossible to doubt that there is a remedy, and it is equally impossible to believe that it is a secret. The idea that some few men, by happy chance or happier temperament, have been given the secret—as if there were some sort of knack or trick of it—is wholly incredible and wrong. Religion must be for all, and the way into its loftiest heights must be by a gateway through which the peoples of the world may pass.

I shall have to lead up to this gateway by a very familiar path. But as this path is strangely unfrequented where it passes into the religious sphere, I must ask your forbearance for dwelling for a moment upon the commonest of common-places.

I. EFFECTS REQUIRE CAUSES.

Nothing that happens in the world happens by chance. God is a God of order. Everything is arranged upon definite principles, and never at random. The world, even the religious world, is governed by law. Character is governed by law. Happiness is governed by law. The Christian experiences are governed by law. Men, forgetting this, expect Rest, Joy, Peace, Faith to drop into their souls from the air like snow or rain. But in point of fact they do not do so; and if they did, they would no less have their origin in previous activities and be controlled by natural laws. Rain and snow do drop from the air, but not without a long previous history. They are the mature effects of former causes. Equally so are Rest and Peace and Joy. They, too, have each a previous history. Storms and winds and calms are not accidents, but brought about by antecedent circumstances. Rest and Peace are but calms in man's inward nature, and arise through causes as definite and as inevitable.

Realize it thoroughly; it is a methodical, not an accidental world. If a housewife turns out a good cake, it is the result of a sound receipt, carefully applied. She cannot mix the assigned ingredients and fire them for the appropriate time without producing the result. It is not she who has made the cake; it is nature. She brings related things together; sets causes at work; these causes bring about the result. She is not a creator, but an intermediary. She does not expect random causes to produce specific effects—random ingredients would only produce random cakes. So it is in the making of Christian experiences. Certain lines are followed; certain effects are the result. These effects cannot but be the result. But the result can never take place without the previous cause. To expect results without antecedents is to expect cakes without ingredients. That impossibility is precisely the almost universal expectation.

Now what I mainly wish to do is to help you firmly to grasp this simple principle of Cause and Effect in the spiritual world. And instead of applying the principle generally to each of the Christian experiences in turn, I shall examine its application to one in some little detail. The one I shall select is Rest. And I think any one who follows the application in this single instance will be able to apply it for himself to all the others.

Take such a sentence as this: African explorers are subject to fevers which cause restlessness and delirium.

Note the expression, "cause restlessness." *Restlessness has a cause.* Clearly, then, any one who wished to get rid of restlessness would proceed at once to deal with the cause. If that were not removed, a doctor might prescribe a hundred things, and all might be taken in turn, without producing the least effect. Things are so arranged in the original planning of the world that certain effects must follow certain causes, and certain causes must be abolished before certain effects can be removed. Certain parts of Africa are inseparably linked with the physical experience called fever; this fever is in turn infallibly linked with a mental experience called restlessness and delirium. To abolish the mental experience the radical method would be to abolish the physical experience, and the way of abolishing the physical experience would be to abolish Africa, or to cease to go there.

Now this holds good for all other forms of Restlessness. Every other form and kind of Restlessness in the world has a definite cause, and the particular kind of Restlessness can only be removed by removing the allotted cause.

All this is also true of Rest. Restlessness has a cause: must not *Rest* have a cause? Necessarily. If it were a chance world we would not expect this; but, being a methodical world, it cannot be otherwise. Rest, physical rest, moral rest, spiritual rest, every kind of rest has a cause, as certainly as restlessness. Now causes are discriminating. There is one kind of cause for every particular effect and no other, and if one particular effect is desired, the corresponding cause must be set in motion. It is no use proposing finely devised schemes, or going through general pious exercises in the hope that somehow Rest will come. The Christian life is not casual, but causal. All nature is a standing protest against the absurdity of expecting to secure spiritual effects, or any effects, without the employment of appropriate causes. The Great Teacher dealt what ought to have been the final blow to this infinite irrelevancy by a single question, "Do men gather grapes of thorns or figs of thistles?"

Why, then, did the Great Teacher not educate His followers fully? Why did He not tell us, for example, how such a thing as Rest might be obtained? The answer is that *He did*. But plainly, explicitly, in so many words? Yes, plainly, explicitly, in so many words. He assigned Rest to its cause, in words with which each of us has been familiar from his earliest childhood.

He begins, you remember—for you at once know the passage I refer to—almost as if Rest could be had without any cause; "Come unto me," He says, "and I will *give* you Rest."

Rest, apparently, was a favor to be bestowed; men had but to come to Him; He would give it to every applicant. But the next sentence takes that all back. The qualification, indeed, is added instantaneously. For what the first sentence seemed to give was next thing to an impossibility. For how, in a literal sense, can Rest be *given*? One could no more give away Rest than he could give away Laughter. We speak of "causing" laughter, which we can do; but we can not give it away. When we speak of "giving" pain, we know perfectly well we can not give pain away. And when we aim at "giving" pleasure, all that we do is to arrange a set of circumstances in such a way as that these shall cause pleasure. Of course there is a sense, and a very wonderful sense, in which a Great Personality breathes upon all who come within its influence an abiding peace and trust. Men can be to other men as the shadow of a great rock in a weary land; much more Christ; much more Christ as Perfect Man; much more still as Savior of the world. But it is not this of which I speak. When Christ said He would give men Rest, He meant simply that He would put them in the way of it. By no act of conveyance would or could He make over His own Rest to them. He could give them HIS RECEIPT for it. That was all. But He would not make it for them. For one thing it was not in His plan to make it for them; for another thing, men were not so planned that it could be made for them; and for yet another thing, it was a thousand times better that they should make it for themselves.

That this is the meaning becomes obvious from the wording of the second sentence: "Learn of me, and ye shall *find* Rest." Rest, (that is to say), is not a thing that can be *given*, but a thing to be *acquired*. It comes not by an act, but by a process. It is not to be found in a happy hour, as one finds a treasure; but slowly, as one finds knowledge. It could indeed be no more found in a moment than could knowledge. A soil has to be prepared for it. Like a fine fruit, it will grow in one climate, and not in another; at one altitude, and not at another. Like all growth it will have an orderly development and mature by slow degrees.

The nature of this slow process Christ clearly defines when He says we are to achieve Rest by *learning*. "Learn of me," He says, "and ye shall find rest to your souls."

Now consider the extraordinary ORIGINALITY OF THIS UTTERANCE.

How novel the connection between these two words "Learn" and "Rest." How few of us have ever associated them—ever thought that Rest was a thing to be learned; ever laid ourselves out for it as we would to learn a language; ever practised it as we would practice the violin? Does it not show how entirely new Christ's teaching still is to the world, that so old and threadbare an aphorism should still be so little known? The last thing most of us would have thought of would have been to associate *Rest* with *Work*.

What must one work at? What is that which if duly learned will find the soul of man in Rest? Christ answers without the least hesitation. He specifies two things—Meekness and Lowliness. "Learn of me," He says, "for I am *meek* and *lowly* in heart."

Now these two things are not chosen at random. To these accomplishments, in a special way, Rest is attached. Learn these, in short, and you have already found Rest. These as they stand are direct causes of Rest; will produce it at once; cannot but produce it at once. And if you think for a single moment, you will see how this is necessarily so, for causes are never arbitrary, and the connection between antecedent and consequent here and everywhere lies deep in the nature of things.

What is the connection, then? I answer by a further question. WHAT ARE THE CHIEF CAUSES OF UNREST? If you know yourself, you will answer—Pride; Selfishness, Ambition. As you look back upon the past years of your life, is it not true that its unhappiness has chiefly come from the succession of personal mortifications and almost trivial disappointments which the intercourse of life has brought you? Great trials come at lengthened intervals, and we rise to breast them; but it is the petty friction of our every-day life with one another, the jar of business or of work, the discord of the domestic circle, the collapse of our ambition, the crossing of our will or the taking down of our conceit, which make inward peace impossible. Wounded vanity, then, disappointed hopes, unsatisfied selfishness—these are the old, vulgar, universal SOURCES OF MAN'S UNREST.

Now it is obvious why Christ pointed out as the two chief objects for attainment the exact opposites of these. To meekness and lowliness these things simply do not exist. They cure unrest by making it impossible. These remedies do not trifle with surface symptoms; they strike at once at removing causes. The ceaseless chagrin of a self-centered life can be removed at once by learning meekness and lowliness of heart. He who learns them is forever proof against it. He lives henceforth a charmed life. Christianity is a fine inoculation, a transfusion of healthy blood into an anæmic or poisoned soul. No fever can attack a perfectly sound body; no fever of unrest can disturb a soul which has breathed the air or learned the ways of Christ.

Men sigh for the wings of a dove that they may fly away and be at Rest. But flying away will not help us. "The Kingdom of God is *within you*." We aspire to the top to look for Rest; it lies at the bottom. Water rests only when it gets to the lowest place. So do men. Hence, *be lowly*. The man who has no opinion of himself at all can never be hurt if others do not acknowledge him. Hence, *be meek*. He who is without expectation cannot fret if nothing comes to him. It is self-evident that these things are so. The lowly man and the meek man are really above all other men, above all other things. They dominate the world because they do not care for it. The miser does not possess gold, gold possesses him. But the meek possess it. "The meek," said Christ, "inherit the earth." They do not buy it; they do not conquer it; but they inherit it.

There are people who go about the world looking out for slights, and they are necessarily miserable, for they find them at every turn—especially the imaginary ones. One has the same pity for such men as for the very poor. They are the morally illiterate. They have had no real education, for they have never learned HOW TO LIVE. Few men know how to live. We grow up at random carrying into mature life the merely animal methods and motives which we had as little children. And it does not occur to us that all this must be changed; that much of it must be reversed; that life is the finest of the Fine Arts; that it has to be learned with lifelong patience, and that the years of our pilgrimage are all too short to master it triumphantly.

Yet this is what Christianity is for—to teach men THE ART OF LIFE. And its whole curriculum lies in one word—"Learn of me." Unlike most education, this is almost purely personal; it is not to be had from books, or lectures or creeds or doctrines. It is a study from the life. Christ never said much in mere words about the Christian graces. He lived them, He was them. Yet we do not merely copy Him. We learn His art by living with Him, like the old apprentices with their masters.

Now we understand it all? Christ's invitation to the weary and heavy-laden is a call to begin life over again upon a new principle—upon His own principle. "Watch my way of doing things," He says; "Follow me. Take life as I take it. Be meek and lowly, and you will find Rest."

I do not say, remember, that the Christian life to every man, or to any man, can be a bed of roses. No educational process can be this. And perhaps if some men knew how much was involved in the simple "learn" of Christ, they would not enter His school with so irresponsible a heart. For there is not only much to learn, but MUCH TO UNLEARN. Many men never go to this school at all till their disposition is already half ruined and character has taken on its fatal set. To learn arithmetic is difficult at fifty—much more to learn Christianity. To learn simply what it is to be meek and lowly, in the case of one who has had no lessons in that in childhood, may cost him half of what he values most on earth. Do we realize, for instance, that the way of teaching humility is generally by *humiliation*? There is probably no other school for it. When a man enters himself as a pupil in such a school it means a very great thing. There is much Rest there, but there is also much Work.

I should be wrong, even though my theme is the brighter side, to ignore the cross and minimize the cost. Only it gives to the cross a more definite meaning, and a rarer value, to connect it thus directly and casually with the growth of the inner life. Our platitudes on the "benefits of affliction" are usually about as vague as our theories of Christian Experience. "Somehow" we believe affliction does us good. But it is not a question of "Somehow." The result is definite, calculable, necessary. It is under the strictest law of cause and effect. The first effect of losing one's fortune, for instance, is humiliation; and the effect of humiliation, as we have just seen, is to make one humble; and the effect of being humble is to produce Rest. It is a roundabout way, apparently, of producing Rest; but Nature generally works by circular processes; and it is not certain that there is any other way of becoming humble, or of finding Rest. If a man could make himself humble to order, it might simplify matters; but we do not find that this happens. Hence we must all go through the mill. Hence death, death to the lower self, is the nearest gate and the quickest road to life.

Yet this is only half the truth. Christ's life outwardly was one of the most troubled lives that was ever lived: tempest and tumult, tumult and tempest, the waves breaking over it all the time till the worn body was laid in the grave. But the inner life was a sea of glass. The great calm was always there. At any moment you might have gone to Him and found Rest. Even when the blood-hounds were dogging Him in the streets of Jerusalem, He turned to His disciples and offered them, as a last legacy, "My peace." Nothing ever for a moment broke the serenity of Christ's life on earth. Misfortune could not reach Him; He had no fortune. Food, raiment, money—fountain-heads of half the world's weariness—He simply did not care for; they played no part in His life; He "took no thought" for them. It was impossible to affect Him by lowering His reputation. He had already made Himself of no reputation. He was dumb before insult. When he was reviled, He reviled not again. In fact, there was NOTHING THAT THE WORLD COULD DO TO HIM that could ruffle the surface of His spirit.

Such living, as mere living, is altogether unique. It is only when we see what it was in Him that we can know what the word Rest means. It lies not in emotions, or in the absence of emotions. It is not a hallowed feeling that comes over us in church. It is not something that the preacher has in his voice. It is not in nature, or in poetry, or in music— though in all these there is soothing. It is the mind at leisure from itself. It is the perfect poise of the soul; the absolute adjustment of the inward man to the stress of all outward things; the preparedness against every emergency; the stability of assured convictions; the eternal calm of an invulnerable faith; the repose of a heart set deep in God. It is the mood of the man who says, with Browning, "God's in His Heaven, all's well with the world."

Two painters each painted a picture to illustrate his conception of rest. The first chose for his scene a still, lone lake among the far-off mountains. The second threw on his canvas a thundering waterfall, with a fragile birch-tree bending over the foam; at the fork of a branch, almost wet with the cataract's spray, a robin sat on its nest. The first was only *Stagnation*; the last was *Rest*. For in Rest there are always two elements—tranquility and energy; silence and turbulence; creation and destruction; fearlessness and fearfulness. This it was in Christ.

It is quite plain from all this that whatever else He claimed to be or to do, He at least KNEW HOW TO LIVE. All this is the perfection of living, of living in the mere sense of passing through the world in the best way. Hence His anxiety to communicate His idea of life to others. He came, He said, to give men life, true life, a more abundant life than they were living; "the life," as the fine phase in the Revised Version has it, "that is life indeed." This is what He Himself possessed, and it was this which He offers to mankind. And hence His direct appeal for all to come to Him who had not made much of life, who were weary and heavy-laden. These He would teach His secret. They, also, should know "the life that is life indeed."

II. WHAT YOKES ARE FOR.

There is still one doubt to clear up. After the statement, "Learn of Me," Christ throws in the disconcerting qualification:

"*Take my yoke* upon you, and learn of Me."

Why, if all this be true, does He call it a *yoke*? Why, while professing to give Rest, does He with the next breath whisper "*burden*"? Is the Christian life, after all, what its enemies take it for—an additional weight to the already great woe of life, some extra punctiliousness about duty, some painful devotion to observances, some heavy restriction and trammeling of all that is joyous and free in the world? Is life not hard and sorrowful enough without being fettered with yet another yoke?

It is astounding how so glaring a misunderstanding of this plain sentence should ever have passed into currency. Did you ever stop to ask what a yoke is really for? Is it to be a burden to the animal which wears it? It is just the opposite. It is to make its burden light. Attached to the oxen in any other way than by a yoke, the plough would be intolerable. Worked by means of a yoke, it is light. A yoke is not an instrument of torture; it is AN INSTRUMENT OF MERCY.

It is not a malicious contrivance for making work hard; it is a gentle device to make hard labor light. It is not meant to give pain, but to save pain. And yet men speak of the yoke of Christ as if it were slavery, and look upon those who wear it as objects of compassion. For generations we have had homilies on "The Yoke of Christ"—some delighting in portraying its narrow exactions; some seeking in these exactions the marks of its divinity; others apologizing for it, and toning it down; still others assuring us that, although it be very bad, it is not to be compared with the positive blessings of Christianity. How many, especially among the young, has this one mistaken phrase driven forever away from the kingdom of God? Instead of making Christ attractive, it makes Him out a taskmaster, narrowing life by petty restrictions, calling for self-denial where none is necessary, making misery a virtue under the plea that it is the yoke of Christ, and happiness criminal because it now and then evades it. According to this conception,

Christians are at best the victims of a depressing fate; their life is a penance; and their hope for the next world purchased by a slow martyrdom in this.

The mistake has arisen from taking the word "yoke" here in the same sense as in the expressions "under the yoke," or "wear the yoke in his youth." But in Christ's illustration it is not the *jugum* of the Roman soldier, but the simple "harness" or "ox-collar" of the Eastern peasant. It is the literal wooden yoke which He, with His own hands in the carpenter shop, had probably often made. He knew the difference between a smooth yoke and a rough one, a bad fit and a good fit; the difference also it made to the patient animal which had to wear it. The rough yoke galled, and the burden was heavy; the smooth yoke caused no pain, and the load was lightly drawn. The badly fitted harness was a misery; the well-fitted collar was "easy."

And what was the "burden"? It was not some special burden laid upon the Christian, some unique infliction that they alone must bear. It was what all men bear. It was simply life, human life itself, the general burden of life which all must carry with them from the cradle to the grave. Christ saw that men took life painfully. To some it was a weariness, to others a failure, to many a tragedy, to all a struggle and a pain. How to carry this burden of life had been the whole world's problem. It is still the whole world's problem. And here is Christ's solution: "Carry it as I do. Take life as I take it. Look at it from My point of view. Interpret it upon My principles. Take My yoke and learn of Me, and you will find it easy. For My yoke is easy, works easily, sits right upon the shoulders, and *therefore* My burden is light."

There is no suggestion here that religion will absolve any man from bearing burdens. That would be to absolve him from living, since it is life itself that is the burden. What Christianity does propose is to make it tolerable.

CHRIST'S YOKE is simply His secret for the alleviation of human life, His prescription for the best and happiest method of living. Men harness themselves to the work and stress of the world in clumsy and unnatural ways. The harness they put on is antiquated. A rough, ill-fitted collar at the best, they make its strain and friction past enduring, by placing it where the neck is most sensitive; and by mere continuous irritation this sensitiveness increases until the whole nature is quick and sore.

This is the origin, among other things, of a disease called "touchiness"—a disease which, in spite of its innocent name, is one of the gravest sources of restlessness in the world. Touchiness, when it becomes chronic, is a morbid condition of the inward disposition. It is self-love inflamed to the acute point; conceit, *with a hair-trigger.* The cure is to shift the yoke to some other place; to let men and things touch us through some new and perhaps as yet unused part of our nature; to become meek and lowly in heart while the old sensitiveness is becoming numb from want of use.

It is the beautiful work of Christianity everywhere to adjust the burden of life to those who bear it, and them to it. It has a perfectly miraculous gift of healing. Without doing any violence to human nature it sets it right with life, harmonizing it with all surrounding things, and restoring those who are jaded with the fatigue and dust of the world to a new grace of living. In the mere matter of altering the perspective of life and changing the proportions of things, its function in lightening the care of man is altogether its own.

The weight of a load depends upon the attraction of the earth. Suppose the attraction of the earth were removed? A ton on some other planet, where the attraction of gravity is less, does not weigh half a ton. Now Christianity removes the attraction of the earth; and this is one way in which it diminishes man's burden. It makes them citizens of another world. What was a ton yester-

day is not half a ton today. So without changing
one's circumstances, merely by offering a wider
horizon and a different standard, it alters the
whole aspect of the world.

Christianity as Christ taught is the truest philosophy of life ever spoken. But let us be quite
sure when we speak of Christianity that we mean
Christ's Christianity. Other versions are either car-
icatures, or exaggerations, or misunderstandings,
or shortsighted and surface readings. For the most
part their attainment is hopeless and the results
wretched. But I care not who the person is, or
through what vale of tears he has passed, or is about
to pass, there is a new life for him along this path.

III. HOW FRUITS GROW.

Were Rest my subject, there are other things I
should wish to say about it, and other kinds of
Rest of which I should like to speak. But that is not
my subject. My theme is that the Christian experiences are not the work of magic, but come under
the law of Cause and Effect. I have chosen Rest
only as a single illustration of the working of that
principle. If there were time I might next run over
all the Christian experiences in turn, and show
the same wide law applies to each; but I think it
may serve the better purpose if I leave this fur-

ther exercise to yourselves. I know no Bible study that you will find more full of fruit, or which will take you nearer to the ways of God, or make the Christian life itself more solid or more sure. I shall add only a single other illustration of what I mean, before I close.

Where does Joy come from? I knew a Sunday scholar whose conception of Joy was that it was a thing made in lumps and kept somewhere in Heaven, and that when people prayed for it, pieces were somehow let down and fitted into their souls. I am not sure that views as gross and material are not often held by people who ought to be wiser. In reality, Joy is as much a matter of Cause and Effect as pain. No one can get Joy by merely asking for it. It is one of the ripest fruits of the Christian life, and, like all fruits, must be grown. There is a very clever trick in India called the mango trick. A seed is put in the ground and covered up, and after diverse incantations a full-blown mango-bush appears within five minutes. I never met any one who knew how the thing was done, but I never met any one who believed it to be anything else than a conjuring trick. The world is pretty unanimous now in its belief in the order-liness of Nature. Men may not know how fruits grow, but they do know that they cannot grow in an hour. Some lives have not even a stalk on which fruits could hang, even if they did grow in an hour. Some have never planted one sound seed of Joy in all their lives; and others who may have planted a germ or two have lived so little in sunshine that they never could come to maturity.

Whence, then, is joy? Christ put His teaching upon this subject into one of the most exquisite of His parables. I should in any instance have appealed to His teaching here, as in the case of Rest, for I do not wish you to think I am speaking words of my own. But it so happens that He has dealt with it in words of unusual fullness.

I need not recall the whole illustration. It is the parable of the Vine. Did you ever think why Christ spoke that parable? He did not merely throw it into space as a fine illustration of general truths. It was not simply a statement of the mystical union, and the doctrine of an indwelling Christ. It was that; but it was more. After He had said it, He did what was not an unusual thing when He was teaching His greatest lessons—He turned to the disciples and said He would tell them why He had spoken it. It was to tell them HOW TO GET JOY.

"These things have I spoken unto you," He said, "that My Joy might remain in you, and that your Joy might be full." It was a purposed and deliberate communication of His SECRET OF HAPPINESS.

Go back over these verses, then, and you will find the Causes of this Effect, the spring, and the only spring, out of which true Happiness comes. I am not going to analyze them in detail. I ask you to enter into the words for yourselves.

Remember, in the first place, that the Vine was the Eastern symbol of Joy. It was its fruit that made glad the heart of man. Yet, however innocent that gladness—for the expressed juice of the grape was the common drink at every peasant's board—the gladness was only a gross and passing thing. This was not true happiness, and the vine of the Palestine vineyards was not the true vine. "*Christ* was the *true* Vine." Here, then, is the ultimate source of Joy. Through whatever media it reaches us, all true Joy and Gladness find their source in Christ.

By this, of course, is not meant that the actual Joy experienced is transferred from Christ's nature, or is something passed on from Him to us. What is passed on is His method of getting it. There is, indeed, a sense in which we can share another's joy or another's sorrow. But that is another matter. Christ is the source of Joy to men in the sense in which He is the source of Rest. His people share His life, and therefore share its consequences, and one of these is Joy. His method of living is one that in the nature of things produces Joy. When

He spoke of His Joy remaining with us He meant in part that the causes which produced it should continue to act. His followers, (that is to say), by *repeating* His life would experience its accompaniments. His Joy, His kind of Joy, would remain with them.

The medium through which this Joy comes is next explained: "He that abideth in Me, the same bringeth forth much fruit." Fruit first, Joy next; the one the cause or medium of the other. Fruit-bearing is the necessary antecedent; Joy both the necessary consequent and the necessary accompaniment. It lay partly in the bearing fruit, partly in the fellowship which made that possible. Partly, that is to say, Joy lay in mere constant living in Christ's presence, with all that that implied of peace, of shelter, and of love; partly in the influence of that Life upon mind and character and will; and partly in the inspiration to live and work for others, with all that that brought of self-riddance and joy in others' gain. All these, in different ways and at different times, are SOURCES OF PURE HAPPINESS.

Even the simplest of them—to do good to other people—is an instant and infallible specific. There is no mystery about Happiness whatever. Put in the right ingredients and it must come out. He that abideth in Him will bring forth much fruit;

and bringing forth much fruit is Happiness. The infallible receipt for Happiness, then, is to do good; and the infallible receipt for doing good is to abide in Christ. The surest proof that all this is a plain matter of Cause and Effect is that men may try every other conceivable way of finding happiness, and they will fail. Only the right cause in each case can produce the right effect.

Then the Christian experiences are our own making? In the same sense in which grapes are our own making and no more. All fruits *grow*— whether they grow in the soil or in the soul; whether they are the fruits of the wild grape or of the True Vine. No man can *make* things grow. He can *get them to grow* by arranging all the circumstances and fulfilling all the conditions. But the growing is done by God. Causes and effects are eternal arrangements, set in the constitution of the world; fixed beyond man's ordering. What man can do is to place himself in the midst of a chain of sequences. Thus he can get things to grow: thus he himself can grow. But the power is the Spirit of God.

What more need I add but this—test the method by experiment. Do not imagine that you have got these things because you know how to get them. As well try to feed upon a cookery book. But I think I can promise that if you try in this simple and natural way, you will not fail. Spend the time you have spent in sighing for fruits in fulfilling the conditions of their growth. The fruits will come, must come. We have hitherto paid immense attention to *effects*, to the mere experiences themselves; we have described them, extolled them, advised them, prayed for them—done everything but find out what *caused* them. Henceforth LET US DEAL WITH CAUSES.

"To be," says Lotze, "is to be in relations." About every other method of living the Christian life there is an uncertainty. About every other method of acquiring the Christian experiences there is a "perhaps." But in so far as this method is the way of nature, it cannot fail. Its guarantee is the laws of the universe—and these are "the Hands of the Living God." THE TRUE VINE. "I am the true vine, and my Father is the husbandman. Every branch in me that beareth not fruit he taketh away; and every branch that beareth fruit, he purgeth it, that it may bring forth more fruit. Now ye are clean through the word which I have spoken unto you. Abide in me, and I in you. As the branch cannot bear fruit of itself, except it abide in the vine; no more can ye, except ye abide in me. I am the vine, ye are the branches: He that abideth in me, and I in him, the same bringeth forth much fruit: for without me ye can do nothing. If a man abide not in me, he is cast forth as a branch, and is withered; and men gather them, and cast them into the fire, and they are burned. If ye abide in me, and my word abide in you, ye shall ask what ye will, and it shall be done unto you. Herein is my Father glorified, that ye bear much fruit; so ye shall be my disciples. As the Father hath loved me, so have I loved you: continue ye in my love. If ye keep my commandments, ye shall abide in my love; even as I have kept my Father's commandments, and abide in his love. These things have I spoken unto you, that my joy might remain in you, and that your joy might be full."

"First!" An Address to Boys

⌐◡

I have three heads to give you. The first is "Geography," the second is "Arithmetic," and the third is "Grammar."

I. Geography

First. Geography tells us where to find places.

Where is the Kingdom of God? It is said that when a Prussian officer was killed in the Franco-Prussian war, a map of France was very often found in his pocket. When we wish to occupy a country, we ought to know its geography. Now, *where* is the Kingdom of God? A boy over there says, "It is in heaven." No; it is not in heaven. Another boy says, "It is in the Bible." No; it is not in the Bible. Another boy says, "It must be in the Church," No; it is not in the Church. Heaven is only the capital of the Kingdom of God; the Bible is the guide-book to it; the Church is the weekly parade of those who belong to it. If you turn to the seventeenth chapter of Luke you will find out where the Kingdom of God really is: "The Kingdom of God is within you"—within *you*. The Kingdom of God is *inside people*.

I remember once taking a walk by the river near where the Falls of Niagara are, and I noticed a remarkable figure walking along the river bank. I had been some time in America. I had seen black men, and red men, and yellow men, and white men; black men, the Negroes; red men, the Indians; yellow men, the Chinese; white men, the Americans. But this man looked quite different in his dress from anything I had ever seen. When he came a little closer, I saw he was wearing a kilt; when he came a little nearer still, I saw that he was dressed exactly like a Highland soldier. When he came quiet near, I said to him:

"What are you doing here?"

"Why should I not be here?" he replied; "don't you know this is British soil? When you cross the river you come into Canada."

This soldier was thousands of miles from England, and yet he was in the Kingdom of England. Wherever there is an English heart beating loyal to the Queen of Britain, there is England. Wherever there is a boy whose heart is loyal to the Kingdom of God, the Kingdom of God is within him.

What is the Kingdom of God? Every Kingdom has its exports, its products. Go down the river here and you will find ships coming in with cotton; you know they come from America. You will find ships with tea; you know they are from China. Ships with wool; you know they come from Australia. Ships with sugar; you know they come from Java.

What comes from the Kingdom of God? Again we must refer to our Guide-book. Turn to Romans, and we shall find what the Kingdom of God is. I will read it: "The Kingdom of God is righteousness, peace, joy"—three things. "The Kingdom of God is righteousness, peace, joy." Righteousness, of course, is just doing what is right. Any boy who does what is *right* has the Kingdom of God within him. Any boy who, instead of being quarrelsome, lives at peace with the other boys, has the Kingdom of God within him. Any boy whose heart is filled with joy because he does what is right, has the Kingdom of God within him. The Kingdom of God is not going to religious meetings, and hearing strange religious experiences; the Kingdom of God is doing what is right—living at peace with all men, being filled with joy in the Holy Ghost.

Boys, if you are going to be Christians, be Christians as boys, and not as your grandmothers. A grandmother has to be a Christian as a grandmother, and that is the right and the beautiful thing for her; but if you cannot read your Bible by the hour as your grandmother can, or delight in meetings as she can, don't think you are necessarily a bad boy. When you are your grandmother's age you will have your grandmother's kind of religion. Meantime, be a Christian as a boy. Live a boy's life. Do the straight thing; seek the kingdom of righteousness and honor and truth. Keep the peace with the boys about you, and be filled with the joy of being a loyal, and simple, and natural, and boy-like servant of Christ.

You can very easily tell a house, or a workshop, or an office where the Kingdom of God is *not*. The first thing you see in that place is that the "straight thing" is not always done. Customers do not get fair play. You are in danger of learning to cheat and to lie. Better a thousand times to starve than to stay in a place where you cannot do what is right.

Or, when you go into your workshop, you find everybody sulky, touchy, and ill-tempered, everybody at daggers-drawn with everybody else, some of the men not on speaking terms with some of the others, and the whole *feel* of the place miserable and unhappy. The Kingdom of God is not there, for *it* is peace. It is the Kingdom of the Devil that is anger, and wrath and malice.

If you want to get the Kingdom of God into your workshop, or into your home, let the quarreling be stopped. Live in peace and harmony and brotherliness with everyone. For the Kingdom of God is a kingdom of brothers. It is a great Society, founded by Jesus Christ, of all the people who try to live like Him, and to make the world better and sweeter and happier. Wherever a boy is trying to do that, in the house or on the street, in the workshop or on the baseball field, there is the Kingdom of God. And every boy, however small or obscure or poor, who is seeking that, is a member of it. You see now, I hope, what the Kingdom is.

II. Arithmetic

I pass, therefore, to the second head; What was it? Arithmetic. Are there any arithmetic words in this text? "Added." What other arithmetic words? "First."

Now, don't you think you could not have anything better to seek "first" than the things I have named to do what is right, to live at peace, and be always making those about you happy? You see at once why Christ tells us to seek these things first—because they are THE BEST WORTH SEEKING.

Do you know anything better than these three things, anything happier, purer, nobler? If you do, seek them first. But if you do not, seek first the Kingdom of God. I do not tell you to be religious. You know that. I do not tell you to seek the Kingdom of God. I tell you to seek the Kingdom of God *first. First.* Not many people do that. They put a little religion into their life—once a week, perhaps. They might just as well let it alone. It is not worth seeking the Kingdom of God unless we seek it *first.*

Suppose you take the helm out of a ship and hang it over the bow, and send that ship to sea, will it ever reach the other side? Certainly not. It will drift about anyhow. Keep religion in its place, and it will take you straight through life and straight to your Father in heaven when life is over. But if you do not put it in its place, you may just as well have nothing to do with it. Religion out of its place in a human life is the most miserable thing in the world. There is nothing that requires so much to be kept in its place as religion, and its place is what? second? third? "First." Boys, *first* the Kingdom of God; make it so that it will be natural to you to think about that the very first thing.

There was a boy in Glasgow apprenticed to a gentleman who made telegraphs. (The gentleman told me this himself.) One day this boy was up on the top of a four-story house with a number of men fixing up a telegraph wire. The work was all but done. It was getting late, and the men said they were going away home, and the boy was to nip off the ends of the wire himself. Before going down they told him to be sure to go back to the workshop, when he was finished, with his master's tools.

"Do not leave any of them lying about, whatever you do," said the foreman.

The boy climbed up the pole and began to nip off the ends of the wire. It was a very cold winter night, and the dusk was gathering. He lost his hold and fell upon the slates, slid down, and then over and over to the ground below. A clothes-rope stretched across the "green" on to which he was just about to fall, caught him on the chest and broke his fall; but the shock was terrible, and he lay unconscious among some clothes upon the green.

An old woman came out; seeing her rope broken and the clothes all soiled, thought the boy was drunk, shook him, scolded him, and went for the policeman. The boy with the shaking came back to consciousness, rubbed his eyes, and got upon his feet. What do you think he did? He staggered, half-blind, up the stairs. He climbed the ladder. He got on to the roof of the house. He gathered up his tools, put them into his basket, took them down, and when he got to the ground again fainted dead away.

Just then the policeman came, saw there was something seriously wrong, and carried him away to the hospital, where he lay for some time. I am glad to say he got better.

What was his first thought at that terrible moment? His duty. He was not thinking of himself; he was thinking about his master. First, the Kingdom of God.

But there is another arithmetic word. What is it? "Added."

You know the difference between *addition* and *subtraction*. Now, that is A VERY IMPORTANT DIFFERENCE in religion, because—and it is a very strange thing—very few people know the difference when they begin to talk about religion. They often tell boys that if they seek the Kingdom of God, everything else is going to be *subtracted* from them. They tell them that they are going to become gloomy, miserable, and will lose everything that makes a boy's life worth living—that they will have to stop baseball and story-books, and become little old men, and spend all their time in going to meetings and in singing hymns.

Now, that is not true. Christ never said anything like that. Christ said we are to "Seek first the Kingdom of God," and EVERYTHING ELSE WORTH HAVING is to be *added* unto us. If there is anything I would like you to remember, it is these two arithmetic words—"first" and "added."

I do not mean by "added" that if you become religious you are all going to become *rich*. Here is a boy, who, in sweeping out the shop tomorrow, finds a quarter lying among the orange boxes. Well, nobody has missed it. He puts it in his pocket, and it begins to burn a hole there. By breakfast time he wishes that money were in his master's pocket. And by-and-by he goes to his master. He says (to *himself*, and not to his master), "I was at the Boys' Brigade yesterday, and I was told to seek *first* that which was right." Then he says to his master:

"Please, sir, here is a quarter that I found upon the floor."

The master puts it in the till. What has the boy got in his pocket? Nothing; *but he has got the Kingdom of God in his heart*. He has laid up treasure in heaven, which is of infinitely more worth than the quarter.

Now, that boy does not find a dollar on his way home. I have known that happen, but that is not what is meant by "adding." It does not mean that God is going to pay him in his own coin, for He pays in better coin.

Yet I remember once hearing of a boy who was paid in both ways. He was very, very poor. He lived in a foreign country, and his mother said to him one day that he must go into the great city and start in business, and she took his coat and cut it open and sewed between the lining and the coat forty golden dinars, which she had saved up for many years to start him in life. She told him to take care of robbers as he went across the desert; and as he was going out of the door she said:

"My boy, I have only two words for you—'Fear God, and never tell a lie.'"

The boy started off, and towards evening he saw glittering in the distance the minarets of the great city. But between the city and himself he saw a cloud of dust. It came nearer. Presently he saw that it was a band of robbers.

One of the robbers left the rest and rode toward him, and said:

"Boy, what have you got?"

The boy looked him in the face said:

"I have forty golden dinars sewed up in my coat."

The robber laughed and wheeled around his horse and went away back. He would not believe the boy.

Presently another robber came and he said:

"Boy, what have you got?"

"Forty golden dinars sewed up in my coat."

The robber said: "The boy is a fool," and wheeled his horse and rode away back.

By and by the robber captain came and he said:

"Boy, what have you got?"

"I have forty golden dinars sewed up in my coat."

The robber dismounted, and put his hand over the boy's breast, felt something round, counted one, two, three, four, five, till he counted out the forty golden coins. He looked the boy in the face and said:

"Why did you tell me that?"

The boy said: "Because of God and my mother."

The robber leaned on his spear and thought and said:

"Wait a moment."

He mounted his horse, rode back to the rest of the robbers, and came back in about five minutes with his dress changed. This time he looked not like a robber, but like a merchant. He took the boy up on his horse and said:

"My boy, I have long wanted to do something for my God and for my mother, and I have this moment renounced my robber's life. I am also a merchant. I have a large business house in the city.

I want you to come and live with me, to teach me about your God; and you will be rich, and your mother some day will come and live with us."

And it all happened. By seeking first the Kingdom of God, all these things were added unto him.

Boys, banish forever from your minds the idea that religion is *subtraction*. It does not tell us to give things up, but rather gives us something so much better that they give themselves up. When you see a boy on the street whipping a top, you know, perhaps, that you could not make that boy happier than by giving him a top, a whip, and half an hour to whip it. But next birthday, when he looks back he says,

"What a goose I was last year to be delighted with a top. What I want now is a baseball bat."

Then when he becomes an old man, he does not care in the least for a baseball bat; he wants rest, and a snug fireside and a newspaper every day. He wonders how he could ever have taken up his thoughts with baseball bats and whipping-tops.

Now, when a boy becomes a Christian, he grows out of the evil things one by one—that is to say, if they are really evil—which he used to set his heart upon; (of course I do not mean baseball bats, for they are not evils); and so instead of telling people to give up things, we are safer to tell them to "seek first the Kingdom of God," and then they will get new things and better things, and THE OLD THINGS WILL DROP OFF of themselves. This is what is meant by the "new heart." It means that God puts into us new thoughts and new wishes, and we become quite different.

III. Grammar

Lastly, and very shortly. What was the third head? "Grammar." Right.

Now, I require a clever boy to answer the next question. What is the verb? "Seek." Very good: "seek." What mood is it in? "Imperative mood." What does that mean? "A command." What is the soldier's first lesson? "Obedience." Have you obeyed this command? Remember the imperative mood of these words, "*Seek* first the Kingdom of God."

This is the command of your King. It *must* be done. I have been trying to show you what a splendid thing it is; what a reasonable thing it is; what a happy thing it is; but beyond all these reasons, it is a thing that *must* be done, because we are *commanded* to do it by our Captain. Now, there is His command to seek *first* the Kingdom of God. Have you done it?

"Well," I know some boys will say, "we are going to have a good time, enjoy life, and then we are going to seek—*last*—the Kingdom of God."

Now, that is mean; it is nothing else than mean for a boy to take all the good gifts that God has given him, and then give him nothing back in return but HIS WASTED LIFE. God wants boys' *lives*, not only their souls. It is for active service that soldiers are drilled, and trained, and fed, and armed. That is why you and I are in the world at all—not to prepare to go out of it some day, but to serve God actively in it *now*. It is monstrous, and shameful, and cowardly to talk of seeking the Kingdom *last*. It is shirking duty, abandoning one's rightful post, playing into the enemy's hand by doing nothing to turn his flank. Every hour a Kingdom is coming in your heart, in your home, in the world near you, be it a Kingdom of Darkness or a Kingdom of Light. You are placed where you are, in a particular business, in a particular street, to help on there the Kingdom of God. You cannot do that when you are old and ready to die. By that time your companions will have fought their fight, and lost or won. If they lose, will you not be sorry that you did not help them? Will you not regret that only at the last you helped the Kingdom of God? Perhaps you will not be able to do it then. And then your life has been lost indeed.

Very few people have the opportunity to seek the Kingdom of God at the end. Christ, knowing all that, knowing that religion was a thing for our life, not merely for our death-bed, has laid this command upon us now: "Seek *first* the Kingdom of God."

I am going to leave you with this text itself. Every boy in the world should obey it.

Boys, before you go to work to-morrow, before you go to sleep to-night, resolve that, God helping you, you are going to seek *first* the Kingdom of God. Perhaps some boys here are deserters; they began once before to serve Christ, and they deserted. Come back again, come back again today! Others have never enlisted at all. Will you not do it now? You are old enough to decide. The grandest moment of a boy's life is that moment when he decides to "*Seek first the Kingdom of God.*"

The Changed Life: The Greatest Need of the World

G od is all for quality; man is for quantity. The immediate need of the world at this moment is not more of us, but, if I may use the expression, a better brand of us. To secure ten men of an improved type would be better than if we had ten thousand more of the average Christians distributed all over the world. There is such a thing in the evangelistic sense as winning the whole world and losing our own soul. And the first consideration is our own life—our own spiritual relations to God—our own likeness to Christ. And I am anxious, briefly, to look at the right and the wrong way of becoming like Christ—of becoming better men: the right and the wrong way of sanctification.

Let me begin by naming, and in part discarding, some processes in vogue already for producing better lives. These processes are far from wrong; in their place they may even be essential. One ventures to disparage them only because they do not turn out the most perfect possible work.

1. The first imperfect method is to rely on RESOLUTION. In will power, in mere spasms of earnestness, there is no salvation. Struggle, effort, even agony, have their place in Christianity, as we shall see; but this is not where they come in.

In mid-Atlantic the Etruria, in which I was sailing, suddenly stopped. Something had gone wrong with the engines. There were five hundred ablebodied men on board the ship. Do you think that if we had gathered together and pushed against the mast we could have pushed it on?

When one attempts to sanctify himself by effort, he is trying to make his boat go by pushing against the mast. He is like a drowning man trying to lift himself out of the water by pulling at the hair of his own head.

Christ held up this method almost to ridicule when He said, "Which of you by taking thought can add a cubit to his stature?" Put down that method forever as being futile.

The one redeeming feature of the self-sufficient method is this—that those who try it find out almost at once that it will not gain the goal.

2. Another experimenter says: "But that is not my method. I have seen the folly of a mere wild struggle in the dark. I work on a principle. My plan is not to waste power on random effort, but to concentrate on a single sin. By taking ONE AT A TIME and crucifying it steadily, I hope in the end to extirpate all."

To this, unfortunately, there are four objections: For one thing, life is too short; the name of sin is legion. For another thing, to deal with individual sins is to leave the rest of the nature for the time untouched. In the third place, a single combat with a special sin does not affect the root and spring of the disease. If you dam up a stream at one place, it will simply overflow higher up. If only one of the channels of sin be obstructed, experience points to an almost certain overflow through some other part of the nature. Partial conversion is almost always accompanied by such moral leakage, for the pent-up energies accumulate to the bursting point, and the last state of that soul may be worse than the first. In the last place, religion does not consist in negatives, in stopping this sin and stopping that. The perfect character can never be produced with a pruning knife.

3. But a third protests: "So be it. I make no attempt to stop sins one by one. My method is just the opposite. I COPY THE VIRTUES one by one."

The difficulty about the copying method is that it is apt to be mechanical. One can always tell an engraving from a picture, an artificial flower from a real flower. To copy virtues one by one has somewhat the same effect as eradicating the vices one by one; the temporary result is an overbalanced and incongruous character. Some one defines a *prig* as "a creature that is over-fed for its size." One sometimes finds Christians of this species—over-fed on one side of their nature, but dismally thin and starved looking on the other. The result, for instance, of copying Humility, and adding it on to an otherwise worldly life, is simply grotesque. A rabid temperance advocate, for the same reason, is often the poorest of creatures, flourishing on a single virtue, and quite oblivious that his Temperance is making a worse man of him and not a better. These are examples of fine virtues spoiled by association with mean companions. Character is a unity, and all the virtues must advance together to make the perfect man.

This method of sanctification, nevertheless, is in the true direction. It is only in the details of execution that it fails.

4. A fourth method I need scarcely mention, for it is a variation on those already named. It is THE VERY YOUNG MAN'S METHOD; and the pure earnestness of it makes it almost desecration to touch it. It is to keep a private note-book with columns for the days of the week, and a list of virtues, with spaces against each for marks. This, with many stern rules for preface, is stored away in a secret place, and from time to time, at night-fall, the soul is arraigned before it as before a private judgment bar.

This living by code was Franklin's method; and I suppose thousands more could tell how they had hung up in their bedrooms, or hid in locked-fast drawers, the rules which one solemn day they drew up to shape their lives.

This method is not erroneous, only somehow its success is poor. You bear me witness that it fails. And it fails generally for very matter-of-fact reasons—most likely because one day we forget the rules.

All these methods that have been named—the self-sufficient method, the self-crucifixion method, the mimetic method, and the diary method—are perfectly human, perfectly natural, perfectly igno-rant, and as they stand perfectly inadequate. It is not argued, I repeat, that they must be abandoned. Their harm is rather that they distract attention from the true working method, and secure a fair result at the expense of the perfect one. What that perfect method is we shall now go on to ask.

I. THE FORMULA OF SANCTIFICATION.

A formula, a receipt for Sanctification—can one seriously speak of this mighty change as if the process were as definite as for the production of so many volts of electricity?

It is impossible to doubt it. Shall a mechanical experiment succeed infallibly, and the one vital experiment of humanity remain a chance? Is corn to grow by method, and character by caprice? If we cannot calculate to a certainty that the forces of religion will do their work, then is religion vain. And if we cannot express the law of these forces in simple words, then is Christianity not the world's religion, but the world's conundrum.

Where, then, shall one look for such a formula? Where one would look for any formula—among the text-books. And if we turn to the text-books of Christianity we shall find a formula for this problem as clear and precise as any in the mechanical sciences. If this simple rule, moreover, be but followed fearlessly, it will yield the result of a perfect character as surely as any result that is guaranteed by the laws of nature.

The finest expression of this rule in Scripture, or indeed in any literature, is probably one drawn up and condensed into a single verse by Paul. You will find it in a letter—the second to the Corinthians—written by him to some Christian people who, in a city which was a byword for depravity and licentiousness, were seeking the higher life. To see the point of the words we must take them from the immensely improved rendering of the Revised translation, for the older Version in this case greatly obscures the sense. They are these:

"We all, with unveiled face reflecting as a mirror the glory of the Lord, are transformed into the same image from glory to glory, even as from the Lord, the Spirit."

Now observe at the outset the entire contradiction of all our previous efforts, in the simple passive: "*We are transformed.*"

We *are changed*, as the Old Version has it—we do not change ourselves. No man can change himself. Throughout the New Testament you will find that wherever these moral and spiritual transformations are described the verbs are in the passive. Presently it will be pointed out that there is a *rationale* in this; but meantime do not toss these words aside as if this passivity denied all human effort or ignored intelligible law. What is implied for the soul here is no more than is everywhere claimed for the body. In physiology the verbs describing the processes of growth are in the passive. Growth is not voluntary; it takes place, it happens, it is wrought upon matter. So here. "Ye must be born again"—we cannot born ourselves. "Be not conformed to this world, but *be ye transformed*"—we are subjects to transforming influence, we do not transform ourselves. Not more certain is it that it is something outside the thermometer that produces a change in the thermometer, than it is SOMETHING OUTSIDE THE SOUL OF MAN that produces a moral change upon him. That he must be susceptible to that change, that he must be a party to it, goes without saying; but that neither his aptitude nor his will can produce it, is equally certain.

Obvious as it ought to seem, this may be to some an almost startling revelation. The change we have been striving after is not to be produced by any more striving. It is to be wrought upon us by the moulding of hands beyond our own. As the branch ascends, and the bud bursts, and the fruit reddens under the co-operation of influences from the outside air, so man rises to the higher stature under invisible pressures from without. The radical defect of all our former methods of sanctification was the attempt to generate from within that which can only be wrought upon us from without. According to the first Law of Motion, every body continues in its state of rest, or of uniform motion in a straight line, except in so far as it may be compelled *by impressed forces* to change that state. This is also a first law of Christianity. Every man's character remains as it is, or continues in the direction in which it is going, until it is compelled *by impressed forces* to change that state. Our failure has been the failure to put ourselves in the way of the impressed forces. There is a clay, and there is a Potter; we have tried to get the clay to mould the clay.

Whence, then, these pressures, and where this Potter? The answer of the formula is—"By reflecting as a mirror the glory of the Lord we are changed." But this is not very clear. What is the "glory" of the Lord, and how can mortal man reflect it, and how can that act as an "impressed force" in moulding him to a nobler form? The word "glory"—the word which has to bear the weight of holding those "impressed forces"—is a stranger in current speech, and our first duty is to seek out its equivalent in working English. It suggests at first a radiance of some kind, something dazzling or glittering, some halo such as the old masters loved to paint round the head of their Ecce Homos. But that is paint, mere matter, the visible symbol of some unseen thing. What is that unseen thing? It is that of all unseen things the most radiant, the most beautiful, the most Divine, and that is *Character*. On earth, in Heaven, there is nothing so great, so glorious as this. The word has many meanings; in ethics it can have but one. Glory is character, and nothing less, and it can be nothing more. The earth is "full of the glory of the Lord," because it is full of His character. The "Beauty of the Lord" is character. "The effulgence of His Glory" is character. "The Glory of the Only Begotten" is character, the character which is "fullness of grace and truth." And when God told His people *His name*, He simply gave them His character, His character which was Himself: "And the Lord proclaimed the name of the Lord . . . the Lord, the Lord God, merciful and gracious, long-suffering and abundant in goodness and truth." Glory then is not something intangible, or ghostly, or transcendental. If it were this, how could Paul ask men to reflect it? Stripped of its physical enswathement it is Beauty, moral and spiritual Beauty, Beauty infinitely real, infinitely exalted, yet infinitely near and infinitely communicable.

With this explanation read over the sentence once more in paraphrase: We all reflecting as a mirror the character of Christ are transformed into the same Image from character to character—

from a poor character to a better one, from a better one to a little better still, from that to one still more complete, until by slow degrees the Perfect Image is attained. Here THE SOLUTION OF THE PROBLEM OF SANCTIFICATION is compressed into a sentence: Reflect the character of Christ, and you will become like Christ. You will be changed, in spite of yourself and unknown to yourself, into the same image from character to character.

(1). All men are reflectors—that is THE FIRST LAW on which this formula is based. One of the aptest descriptions of a human being is that he is a mirror. As we sat at table to-night the world in which each of us lived and moved throughout this day was focused in the room. What we saw when we looked at one another was not one another, but one another's world. We were an arrangement of mirrors. The scenes we saw were all reproduced; the people we met walked to and fro; they spoke, they bowed, they passed us by, did everything over again as if it had been real. When we talked, we were but looking at our own mirror and describing what flitted across it; our listening was not hearing, but seeing—we but looked on our neighbor's mirror.

All human intercourse is a seeing of reflections. I meet a stranger in a railway carriage. The cadence of his first words tells me he is English and comes from Yorkshire. Without knowing it he has reflected his birthplace, his parents, and the long history of their race. Even physiologically he is a mirror. His second sentence records that he is a politician, and a faint inflection in the way he pronounces *The Times* reveals his party. In his next remarks I see reflected a whole world of experiences. The books he has read, the people he has met, the companions he keeps, the influences that have played upon him and made him the man he is—these are all registered there by a pen which lets nothing pass, and whose writing can NEVER BE BLOTTED OUT.

What I am reading in him meantime he also is reading in me; and before the journey is over we could half write each other's lives. Whether we like it or not, we live in glass houses. The mind, the memory, the soul, is simply a vast chamber panelled with looking-glass. And upon this miraculous arrangement and endowment depends the capacity of mortal souls to "reflect the character of the Lord."

(2). But this is not all. If all these varied reflections from our so-called secret life are patent to the world, how close the writing, complete the record within the soul itself! For the influences we meet are not simply held for a moment on the polished surface and thrown off again into space.

Each is retained where first it fell, and stored up in the soul forever.

THIS LAW OF ASSIMILATION is the second, and by far the most impressive truth which under-lies the formula of sanctification—the truth that men are not only mirrors, but that these mirrors, so far from being mere reflectors of the fleeting things they see, transfer into their own inmost substance, and hold in permanent preservation the things that they reflect.

No one knows how the soul can hold these things. No one knows how the miracle is done. No phenomenon in nature, no process in chemis-try, no chapter in necromancy can ever help us to begin to understand this amazing operation. For, think of it, the past is not only *focused* there, in a man's soul, it *is* there. How could it be reflected from there if it were not there? All things that he has ever seen, known, felt, believed of the sur-rounding world are now within him, have become part of him, in part are him—he has been changed into their image. He may deny it, he may resent it, but they are there. They do not adhere to him, they are transfused through him. He cannot alter or rub them out. They are not in his memory, they are in *him*. His soul is as they have filled it, made it, left it. These things, these books, these events, these influences are his makers. In their hands are life and death, beauty and deformity. When once the image or likeness of any of these is fairly presented to the soul, no power on earth can hinder two things happening—it must be absorbed into the soul and forever reflected back again from character.

Upon these astounding yet perfectly obvious psychological facts, Paul bases his doctrine of sanctification. He sees that character is a thing built up by slow degrees, that it is hourly changing for better or for worse according to the images which flit across it. One step further and the whole length and breadth of the application of these ideas to the central problem of religion will stand before us.

II. THE ALCHEMY OF INFLUENCE.

If events change men, much more persons. No man can meet another on the street without making some mark upon him. We say we exchange words when we meet; what we exchange is souls. And when intercourse is very close and very frequent, so complete is this exchange that recognizable bits of the one soul begin to show in the other's nature, and the second is conscious of a similar and growing debt to the first.

Now, we become like those whom we habitually reflect. I could prove from science that applies even to the physical framework of animals—that they are influenced and organically changed by the environment in which they live.

This mysterious approximating of two souls, who has not witnessed? Who has not watched some old couple come down life's pilgrimage hand in hand, with such gentle trust and joy in one another that their very faces wore the self-same look? These were not two souls; it was a composite soul. It did not matter to which of the two you spoke, you would have said the same words to either. It was quite indifferent which replied, each would have said the same. Half a century's *reflecting* had told upon them; they were changed into the same image. It is the Law of Influence that *we become like those whom we habitually reflect*: these had become like because they habitually reflected. Through all the range of literature, of history, and biography this law presides. Men are all mosaics of other men. There was a savor of David about Jonathan, and a savor of Jonathan about David. Metempsychosis is a fact. George Eliot's message to the world was that men and women make men and women. The Family, the cradle of mankind, has no meaning apart from this. Society itself is nothing but a rallying point for these omnipotent forces to do their work. On the doctrine of Influence, in short, the whole vast pyramid of humanity is built.

But it was reserved for Paul to make the supreme application of the Law of Influence. It was a tremendous inference to make, but he never hesitated. He himself was a changed man; he knew exactly what had done it; IT WAS CHRIST.

On the Damascus road they met, and from that hour his life was absorbed in His. The effect could not but follow—on words, on deeds, on career, on creed. The "impressed forces" did their vital work. He became like Him Whom he habitually loved. "So we all," he writes, "reflecting as a mirror the glory of Christ, are changed into the same image."

Nothing could be more simple, more intelligible, more natural, more supernatural. It is an analogy from an every-day fact. Since we are what we are by the impacts of those who surround us, those who surround themselves with the highest will be those who change into the highest. There are some men and some women in whose company we are ALWAYS AT OUR BEST.

While with them we cannot think mean thoughts or speak ungenerous words. Their mere presence is elevation, purification, sanctity. All the best stops in our nature are drawn out by their intercourse, and we find a music in our souls that was never there before. Suppose even *that* influence prolonged through a month, a year, a lifetime, and what could not life become? Here, even on the common plane of life, talking our language, walking our streets, working side by side, are sanctifiers of souls; here, breathing through common clay, is Heaven; here, energies charged even through a temporal medium with the virtue of regeneration. If to live with men, diluted to the millionth degree with the virtue of the Highest, can exalt and purify the nature, what bounds can be set to the influence of Christ? To live with Socrates—with unveiled face—must have made one wise; with Aristides, just. Francis Assisi must have made one gentle; Savonarola, strong. But to have lived with Christ must have made one like Christ: that is to say, *A Christian.*

As a matter of fact, to live with Christ did produce this effect. It produced it in the case of Paul. And during Christ's lifetime the experiment was tried in an even more startling form. A few raw, unspiritual, uninspiring men, were admitted to the inner circle of His friendship. The change began at once. Day by day we can almost see the first disciple grow. First there steals over them the faintest possible adumbration of His character, and occasionally, very occasionally, they do a thing or say a thing that they could not have done or said had they not been living there. Slowly the spell of His Life deepens. Reach after reach of their nature is overtaken, thawed, subjugated, sanctified. Their manner softens, their words become more gentle, their conduct more unselfish. As swallows who have found a summer, as frozen buds the spring, their starved humanity bursts into a fuller life. They do not know how it is, but they are different men.

One day they find themselves like their Master, going about and doing good. To themselves it is unaccountable, but they cannot do otherwise. They were not told to do it, it came to them to do it. But the people who watch them know well how to account for it—"They have been," they whisper, "with Jesus." Already even, the mark and seal of His character is upon them—"They have been with Jesus." Unparalleled phenomenon, that these poor fishermen should remind other men of Christ! Stupendous victory and mystery of REGENERATION that mortal men should suggest *God* to the world!

There is something almost melting in the way His contemporaries, and John especially, speak of the influence of Christ. John lived himself in daily wonder at Him; he was overpowered, over-awed, entranced, transfigured. To his mind it was impossible for any one to come under this influence and ever be the same again. "Whosoever abideth in

Him sinneth not," he said. It was inconceivable that he should sin, as inconceivable as that ice should live in a burning sun, or darkness coexist with noon. If any one did sin, it was to John the simple proof that he could never have met Christ. "Whosoever sinneth," he exclaims, "hath not seen *Him*, neither known *Him*." Sin was abashed in this Presence. Its roots withered. Its sway and victory were forever at an end.

But these were His contemporaries. It was easy for *them* to be influenced by Him, for they were every day and all the day together. But how can we mirror that which we have never seen? How can all this stupendous result be produced by a Memory, by the scantiest of all Biographies, by One who lived and left this earth eighteen hundred years ago? How can modern men to-day make Christ, the absent Christ, their most constant companion still?

The answer is that FRIENDSHIP IS A SPIRITUAL THING. It is independent of Matter, or Space, or Time. That which I love in my friend is not that which I see. What influences me in my friend is not his body but his spirit. He influences me about as much in his absence as in his presence. It would have been an ineffable experience truly to have lived at that time—

"I think when I read the sweet story of old,
How when Jesus was here among men,
He took little children like lambs to His fold,
I should like to have been with Him then.

"I wish that His hand had been laid on my head,
That His arms had been thrown around me,
And that I had seen His kind look when he said,
'Let the little ones come unto me.'"

And yet, if Christ were to come into the world again, few of us probably would ever have a chance of seeing Him. Millions of her subjects in the little country of England have never seen their own Queen. And there would be millions of the subjects of Christ who could never get within speaking distance of Him if He were here. We remember He said: "It is expedient for you (not *for Me*) that I go away"; because by going away He could really be nearer to us than He would have been if He had stayed here. It would be geographically and physically impossible for most of us to be influenced by His person had He remained. And so our communion with Him is a spiritual companionship; but not different from most companionships, which, when you press them down to the roots, you will find to be essentially spiritual.

All friendship, all love, human and Divine, is purely spiritual. It was after He was risen that He influenced even the disciples most. Hence, in reflecting the character of Christ, it is no real obstacle that we may never have been in visible contact with Himself.

There lived once a young girl whose perfect grace of character was the wonder of those who knew her. She wore on her neck a gold locket which no one was ever allowed to open. One day, in a moment of unusual confidence, one of her companions was allowed to touch its spring and learn its secret. She saw written these words— *"Whom having not seen I love."*

That was the secret of her beautiful life. She had been changed into the Same Image.

Now this is not imitation, but a much deeper thing. Mark this distinction, for the difference in the process, as well as in the result, may be as great as that between a photograph secured by the infallible pencil of the sun, and the rude outline from a school-boy's chalk. Imitation is mechanical, reflection organic. The one is occasional, the other habitual. In the one case, man comes to God and imitates him; in the other, God comes to man and imprints Himself upon him. It is quite true that there is an imitation of Christ which amounts to reflection. But Paul's term includes all that the other holds, and is open to no mistake.

What, then, is the practical lesson? It is obvious. "Make Christ your most constant companion"—this is what it practically means for us. Be more under His influence than under any other influence. Ten minutes spent in His society every day, two minutes if it be face to face, and heart to heart, will make the whole day different. Every character has an inward spring,—let Christ be it. Every action has a key-note,—let Christ set it.

Yesterday you got a certain letter. You sat down and wrote a reply which almost scorched the paper. You picked the cruelest adjectives you knew and sent it forth, without a pang to do its ruthless work. You did that because your life was set in the wrong key. You began the day with the mirror placed at the wrong angle.

Tomorrow at day-break, turn it towards Him, and even to your enemy the fashion of your countenance will be changed. Whatever you then do, one thing you will find you could not do—you could not write that letter. Your first impulse may be the same, your judgment may be unchanged, but if you try it the ink will dry on your pen, and you will rise from your desk an unavenged, but a greater and more Christian man. Throughout the whole day your actions, down to the last detail, will do homage to that early vision.

Yesterday you thought mostly about yourself. Today the poor will meet you, and you will feed them. The helpless, the tempted, the sad, will throng about you, and each you will befriend. Where were all these people yesterday? Where they are today, but you did not see them. It is in reflected light that the poor are seen. But your soul today is NOT AT THE ORDINARY ANGLE. "Things which are not seen" are visible. For a few short hours you live the Eternal Life. The eternal life, the life of faith, is simply the life of a higher vision. Faith is an attitude—a mirror set at the right angle.

When tomorrow is over, and in the evening you review it, you will wonder how you did it. You will not be conscious that you strove for anything, or imitated anything, or crucified anything. You will be conscious of Christ; that He was with you, that without compulsion you were yet compelled; that without force, or noise, or proclamation, the revolution was accomplished. You do not congratulate yourself as one who has done a mighty deed, or achieved a personal success, or stored up a fund of "Christian experience" to ensure the same result again. What you are conscious of is "the glory of the Lord." And what the world is conscious of, if the result be a true one, is also "the glory of the Lord." In looking at a mirror one does not see the mirror, or think of it, but only of what it reflects. For a mirror never calls the attention to itself— except when there are flaws in it.

Let me say a word or two more about the effects which necessarily must follow from this contact, or fellowship, with Christ. I need not quote the texts upon the subject—the texts about abiding in Christ. "He that abideth in Him sinneth not." You cannot sin when you are standing in front of Christ. You simply cannot do it. Again: "If ye abide in Me, and My words abide in you, ye shall ask what ye will, and it shall be done unto you." Think of that! That is another inevitable consequence. And there is yet another: "He that abideth in Me, the same bringeth forth much fruit." Sinlessness— answered prayer—much fruit.

But in addition to these things, see how many of the highest Christian virtues and experiences necessarily flow from the assumption of that atti-tude toward Christ. For instance, the moment you assume that relation to Christ you begin to know what the *child-spirit* is. You stand before Christ, and He becomes your Teacher, and you instinctively become docile. Then you learn also to become *charitable* and *tolerant*; because you are learning of Him, and He is "meek and lowly in heart," and you catch that spirit. That is a bit of His character being reflected into yours. Instead of being critical and self-asserting, you become humble and have the mind of a little child.

I think, further, the only way of learning what *faith* is is to know Christ and be in His company. You hear sermons about the nine different kinds of faith—distinctions drawn between the right kind of faith and the wrong—and sermons telling you how to get faith. So far as I can see, there is ONLY ONE WAY in which faith is got, and it is the same in the religious world as it is in the world of men and women. I learn to trust you, my brother, just as I get to know you, and neither more nor less; and you get to trust me just as you get to know me. I do not trust you as a stranger, but as I come into contact with you, and watch you, and live with you, I find out that you are trustworthy, and I come to trust myself to you, and to lean upon you. But I do not do that to a stranger.

The way to trust Christ is to know Christ. You cannot help trusting Him then. You are changed. By knowing Him faith is begotten in you, as cause and effect. To trust Him without knowing Him as thousands do, is not faith, but credulity. I believe a great deal of prayer for faith is thrown away. What we should pray for is that we may be able to fulfill the condition, and when we have fulfilled the condition, the faith necessarily follows. The way, therefore, to increase our faith is to increase our intimacy with Christ. We trust Him more and more the better we know Him.

And then another immediate effect of this way of sanctifying the character is the tranquillity that it brings over the Christian life. How disturbed and distressed and anxious Christian people are about their growth in grace! Now, the moment you give that over into Christ's care—the moment you see that you are *being* changed—that anxiety passes away. You see that it must follow by an inevitable process and by a natural law if you fulfill the simple condition; so that peace is the reward of that life and fellowship with Christ.

Many other things follow. A man's usefulness depends to a large extent upon his fellowship with Christ. That is obvious. Only Christ can influence the world; but all that the world sees of Christ is what it sees of you and me. Christ said: "The world seeth Me no more, but ye see Me." You see Him, and standing in front of Him reflect Him, and the world sees the reflection. It cannot see Him. So that a Christian's usefulness depends solely upon that relationship.

Now, I have only pointed out a few of the things that follow from the standing before Christ—from the abiding in Christ. You will find, if you run over the texts about abiding in Christ, many other things will suggest themselves in the same relations. Almost everything in Christian experience and character follows, and follows necessarily, from standing before Christ and reflecting his character. But the supreme consummation is that we are changed into *the same image*, "even as by the Lord the Spirit." That is to say, that in some way, unknown to us, but possibly not more mysterious than the doctrine of personal influence, we are changed into the image of Christ.

This method cannot fail. I am not setting before you an opinion or a theory, but this is A CERTAINLY SUCCESSFUL MEANS of sanctification. "We all, with unveiled face, reflecting in a mirror the glory of Christ (the character of Christ) assuredly—without any miscarriage—without any possibility of miscarriage—are changed into the same image." It is an immense thing to be anchored in some great principle like that. Emerson says: "The hero is the man who is immovably centered." Get immovably centered in that doctrine of sanctification. Do not be carried away by the hundred and one theories of sanctification that are floating about in religious literature of the country at the present time; but go to the bottom of the thing for yourself, and see the *rationale* of it for yourself, and you will come to see that it is a matter of cause and effect, and that if you will fulfill the condition laid down by Christ, the effect must follow by a natural law.

What a prospect! To be changed into the same image. Think of that! That is what we are here for. That is what we are elected for. Not to be saved, in the common acceptation, but "whom He did foreknow He also did predestinate to be conformed to the image of His Son." Not merely to be saved, but *to be conformed to the image of His Son.* Conserve that principle. And as we must spend time in cultivating our earthly friendships if we are to have their blessings, so we must SPEND TIME in cultivating the fellowship and companionship of Christ. And there is nothing so much worth taking into our lives as a profounder sense of what is to be had by living in communion with Christ, and by getting nearer to Him. It will matter much if we take away with us some of the thoughts about theology, and some of the new light that has been shed upon the text of Scripture; it will matter infinitely more if our fellowship with the Lord Jesus become a little closer, and our theory of holy living a little more rational. And then as we go forth, men will take knowledge of us, that we have been with Jesus, and as we reflect Him upon them, they will begin to be changed into the same image.

It seems to me the preaching is of infinitely smaller account than the life which mirrors Christ. That is bound to tell; without speech or language—like the voices of the stars. It throws out its impressions on every side. The one simple thing we have to do is to be there—in the right relation; to go through life hand in hand with Him; to have Him in the room with us, and keeping us company wherever we go; to depend upon Him and lean upon Him, and so have His life reflected in the fullness of its beauty and perfection into ours.

III. THE FIRST EXPERIMENT.

Then you reduce religion to a common Friendship? A common Friendship—who talks of a *common* Friendship? There is no such thing in the world.

On earth no word is more sublime. Friendship is the nearest thing we know to what religion is. God is love. And to make religion akin to Friendship is simply to give it the highest expression conceivable by man. But if by demurring to "a common friendship" is meant a protest against the greatest and the holiest in religion being spoken of in intelligible terms, then I am afraid the objection is all too real. Men always look for a mystery when one talks of sanctification, some mystery apart from that which must ever be mysterious wherever Spirit works. It is thought some peculiar secret lies behind it, some occult experience which only the initiated know. Thousands of persons go to church every Sunday hoping to solve this mystery. At meetings, at conferences, many a time they have reached what they thought was the very brink of it, but somehow no further revelation came. Poring over religious books, how often were they not within a paragraph of it; the next page, the next sentence, would discover all, and they would be borne on a flowing tide forever. But nothing happened. The next sentence and the next page were read, and still it eluded them; and though the promise of its coming kept faithfully up to the end, the last chapter found them still pursuing.

Why did nothing happen? Because there was nothing to happen—nothing of the kind they were looking for. Why did it elude them? Because there was no "it." When shall we learn that the pursuit of holiness is simply THE PURSUIT OF CHRIST? When shall we substitute for the "it" of a fictitious aspiration, the approach to a Living Friend? Sanctity is in character and not in moods; Divinity in our own plain calm humanity, and in no mystic rapture of the soul.

And yet there are others who, for exactly a contrary reason, will find scant satisfaction here.

Their complaint is not that a religion expressed in terms of Friendship is too homely, but that it is still too mystical. To "abide" in Christ, to "make Christ our most constant companion," is to them the purest mysticism. They want something absolutely tangible and absolutely direct. These are not the poetical souls who seek a sign, a mysticism in excess, but the prosaic natures whose want is mathematical definition in details. Yet it is perhaps not possible to reduce this problem to much more rigid elements. The beauty of Friendship is its infinity. One can never evacuate life of mysticism. Home is full of it, love is full of it, religion is full of it. Why stumble at that in the relation of man to Christ which is natural in the relation of man to man?

If any one cannot conceive or realize a mystical relation with Christ, perhaps all that can be done is to help him to step on to it by still plainer analogies from common life. How do I know Shakespeare or Dante? By communing with their words and thoughts. Many men know Dante better than their own fathers. He influences them more. As a spiritual presence he is more near to them, as a spiritual force more real. Is there any reason why a greater than Shakespeare or Dante, who also walked this earth, who left great words behind Him, who has greater works everywhere in the world now, should not also instruct, inspire and mould the characters of men? I do not limit Christ's influence to this: it is this, and it is more. But Christ, so far from resenting or discouraging this relation of Friendship, Himself proposed it. "Abide in me" was almost His last word to the world. And He partly met the difficulty of those who feel its intangibleness by adding the practical clause, "If ye abide in Me, *and My words abide in you*."

Begin with His words. Words can scarcely ever be long impersonal. Christ himself was a Word, a word made Flesh. Make His words flesh; do them, live them, and you must live Christ. "*He that keepeth My Commandments*, he it is that loveth Me." Obey Him and you must love Him. Abide in Him, and you must obey Him. *Cultivate* His Friendship. Live after Christ, in His Spirit, as in His Presence, and it is difficult to think what more you can do. Take this at least as a first lesson, as introduction.

If you cannot at once and always feel the play of His life upon yours, watch for it also indirectly. "The whole earth is full of the character of the Lord." Christ is the Light of the world, and much of his Light is reflected from things in the world— even from clouds. Sunlight is stored in every leaf, from leaf through coal, and it comforts us thence when days are dark and we cannot see the sun. Christ shines through men, through books, through history, through nature, music, art. Look for Him there. "Every day one should either look at a beautiful picture, or hear beautiful music, or read a beautiful poem." The real danger of mysticism is not making it broad enough.

Do not think that nothing is happening because you do not see yourself grow, or hear the whir of the machinery. All great things grow noiselessly. You can see a mushroom grow, but never a child. Paul said for the comforting of all slowly perfecting souls that they grew "from character to character." "The inward man," he says elsewhere, "is renewed from day to day." All thorough work is slow; all true development by minute, slight and insensible metamorphoses. The higher the structure, moreover, the slower the progress. As the biologist runs his eye over the long Ascent of Life, he sees the lowest forms of animals develop in an hour; the next above these reach maturity in a day; those higher still take weeks or months to perfect; but the few at the top demand the long experiment of years. If a child and an ape are born on the same day, the last will be in full possession of its faculties and doing the active work of life before the child has left its cradle. Life is the cradle of eternity. As the man is to the animal in the slowness of his evolution, so is the spiritual man to the natural man. Foundations which have to bear the weight of an eternal life must be surely laid. Character is to wear forever; who will wonder or grudge that it cannot be developed in a day?

To await the growing of a soul, nevertheless, is an almost Divine act of faith. How pardonable, surely, the impatience of deformity with itself, of a consciously despicable character standing before Christ, wondering, yearning, hungering to be like that! Yet must one trust the process fearlessly and without misgiving. "The Lord the Spirit" will do His part. The tempting expedient is, in haste for abrupt or visible progress, to try some method less spiritual, or to defeat the end by watching for effects instead of keeping the eye on the Cause. A photograph prints from the negative only while exposed to the sun. While the artist is looking to see how it is getting on he simply stops the getting on. Whatever of wise supervision the soul may need, it is certain it can never be over-exposed, or that, being exposed, anything else in the world can improve the result or quicken it. The creation of a new heart, the renewing of a right spirit, is an omnipotent work of God. Leave it to the Creator. "He which hath begun a good work in you will perfect it unto that day."

No man, nevertheless, who feels the worth and solemnity of what is at stake will be careless as to his progress. To become LIKE CHRIST is the only thing in the world worth caring for, the thing before which every ambition of man is folly, and all lower achievement vain.

Those only who make this quest the supreme desire and passion of their lives can ever begin to hope to reach it. If, therefore, it has seemed up to this point as if all depended on passivity, let me now assert, with conviction more intense, that all depends on activity. A religion of effortless adoration may be a religion for an angel, but never for a man. Not in the contemplative, but in the active, lies true hope; not in rapture, but in reality, lies true life; not in the realm of ideals, but among tangible things, is man's sanctification wrought. Resolution, effort, pain, self-crucifixion, agony—all the things already dismissed as futile in themselves, must now be restored to office, and a tenfold responsibility laid upon them. For what is their office? Nothing less than to move the vast inertia of the soul, and place it, and keep it where the spiritual forces will act upon it. It is to rally the forces of the will, and keep the surface of the mirror bright and ever in position. It is to uncover the face which is to look at Christ, and draw down the veil when unhallowed sights are near.

You have, perhaps, gone with an astronomer to watch him photograph the spectrum of a star. As you enter the dark vault of the observatory you saw him begin by lighting a candle. To see the star with? No; but to adjust the instrument to see the star with. It was the star that was going to take the photograph; it was, also, the astronomer. For a long time he worked in the dimness, screwing tubes and polishing lenses and adjusting reflectors, and only after much labor the finely focused instrument was brought to bear. Then he blew out the light, and left the star to do its work upon the plate alone.

The day's task for the Christian is to bring his instrument to bear. Having done that he may blow out his candle. All the evidences of Christianity which have brought him there, all aids to Faith, all acts of worship, all the leverages of the Church, all Prayer and Meditation, all girding of the Will— these lesser processes, these candle-light activities for that supreme hour, may be set aside. But, remember, it is but for an hour. The wise man will be he who quickest lights his candle, the wisest he who never lets it out. Tomorrow, the next moment, he, a poor, darkened, blurred soul, may need it again to focus the Image better, to take a mote off the lens, to clear the mirror from a breath with which the world has dulled it.

No readjustment is ever required on behalf of the Star. That is one great fixed point in this shifting universe. But *the world moves.* And each day, each hour, demands a further motion and readjustment for the soul. A telescope in an observatory follows a star by clockwork, but the clockwork of the soul is called *the Will.* Hence, while the soul in passivity reflects the Image of the Lord, the Will in intense activity holds the mirror in position lest the drifting motion of the world bear it beyond the line of vision. To "follow Christ" is largely to keep the soul in such position as will allow for the motion of the earth. And this calculated counteracting of the movements of the world, this holding of the mirror exactly opposite to the Mirrored, this steadying of the faculties unerringly through cloud and earthquake, fire and sword, is the stupendous co-operating labor of the Will. It is all man's work. It is all Christ's work. In practice it is both; in theory it is both. But the wise man will say in practice, "It depends upon myself."

In the Gallerie des Beaux Arts in Paris there stands a famous statue. It was the last work of a great genius, who, like many a genius, was very poor and lived in a garret, which served as a studio and sleeping-room alike. When the statue was all but finished, one midnight a sudden frost fell upon Paris. The sculptor lay awake in the fireless room and thought of the still moist clay, thought how the water would freeze in the pores and destroy in an hour the dream of his life. So the old man rose from his couch and heaped the bed-clothes reverently round his work. In the morning when the neighbors entered the room the sculptor was dead, but the statue was saved!

The Image of Christ that is forming within us— that is life's one charge. Let every project stand aside for that. The spirit of God who brooded upon the waters thousands of years ago, is busy now creating men, within these commonplace lives of ours, in the image of God. "Till Christ be formed," no man's work is finished, no religion crowned, no life has fulfilled its end. Is the infinite task begun? When, how, are we to be different? Time cannot change men. Death cannot change men. Christ can. Wherefore *put on Christ.*

Dealing with Doubt

There is a subject which I think workers amongst young men cannot afford to keep out of sight—I mean the subject of "Doubt." We are forced to face that subject. We have no choice. I would rather let it alone; but every day of my life I meet men who doubt, and I am quite sure that most Christian workers among men have innumerable interviews every year with men who raise skeptical difficulties about religion.

Now it becomes a matter of great practical importance that we should know how to deal wisely with these. Upon the whole, I think these are the best men in the country. I speak of my own country. I speak of the universities with which I am familiar, and I say that the men who are perplexed,—the men who come to you with serious and honest difficulties,—are the best men. They are men of intellectual honesty, and cannot allow themselves to be put to rest by words, or phrases, or traditions, or theologies, but who must get to the bottom of things for themselves. And if I am not mistaken, CHRIST WAS VERY FOND of these men. The outsiders always interested Him, and touched Him. The orthodox people—the Pharisees—He was much less interested in. He went with publicans and sinners—with people who were in revolt against the respectability, intellectual and religious, of the day. And following Him, we are entitled to give sympathetic consideration to those whom He loved and took trouble with.

First, let me speak for a moment or two about THE ORIGIN OF DOUBT. In the first place, *we are born questioners*. Look at the wonderment of a little child in its eyes before it can speak. The child's great word when it begins to speak is, "Why?" Every child is full of every kind of question, about every kind of thing, that moves, and shines, and changes, in the little world in which it lives.

That is the incipient doubt in the nature of man. Respect doubt for its origin. It is an inevitable thing. It is not a thing to be crushed. It is a part of man as God made him. Heresy is truth in the making, and doubt is the prelude of knowledge.

Secondly: *The world is a Sphinx.* It is a vast riddle—an unfathomable mystery; and on every side there is temptation to questioning. In every leaf, in every cell of every leaf, there are a hundred problems. There are ten good years of a man's life in investigating what is in a leaf, and there are five good years more in investigating the things that are in the things that are in the leaf. God has planned the world to incite men to intellectual activity.

Thirdly: *The instrument with which we attempt to investigate truth is impaired.* Some say it fell, and the glass is broken. Some say prejudice, heredity, or sin, have spoiled its sight, and have blinded our eyes and deadened our ears. In any case the instruments with which we work upon truth, even in the strongest men, are feeble and inadequate to their tremendous task.

And in the fourth place, *all religious truths are doubtable.* There is no absolute truth for any one of them. Even that fundamental truth—the existence of a God—no man can prove by reason. The ordinary proof for the existence of God involves either an assumption, argument in a circle, or a contradiction. The impression of God is kept up by experience, not by logic. And hence, when the experimental religion of a man, of a community, or of a nation wanes, religion wanes—their idea of God grows indistinct, and that man, community or nation becomes infidel.

Bear in mind, then, that all religious truths are doubtable—even those which we hold most strongly.

What does this brief account of the origin of doubt teach us? It teaches us GREAT INTELLEC-TUAL HUMILITY.

It teaches us sympathy and toleration with all men who venture upon the ocean of truth to find out a path through it for themselves. Do you sometimes feel yourself thinking unkind things about your fellow-students who have intellectual difficulty? I know how hard it is always to feel sympathy and toleration for them; but we must address ourselves to that most carefully and most religiously. If my brother is shortsighted I must not abuse him or speak against him; I must pity him, and if possible try to improve his sight, or to make things that he is to look at so bright that he can-not help seeing. But never let us think evil of men who do not see as we do. From the bottom of our hearts let us pity them, and let us take them by the hand and spend time and thought over them, and try to lead them to the true light.

What has been THE CHURCH'S TREAT-MENT OF DOUBT in the past? It has been very simple. "There is a heretic. Burn him!" That is all. "There is a man who has gone off the road. Bring him back and torture him!"

We have got past that physically; have we got past it morally? What does the modern Church say to a man who is skeptical? Not "Burn him!" but "Brand him!" "Brand him!"—call him a bad name. And in many countries at the present time, a man who is branded as a heretic is despised, tabooed and put out of religious society, much more than if he had gone wrong in morals. I think I am speaking within the facts when I say that a man who is unsound is looked upon in many communities with more suspicion and with more pious horror than a man who now and then gets drunk. "Burn him!" "Brand him!" "Excommunicate him!" That has been the Church's treatment of doubt, and that is perhaps to some extent the treatment which we ourselves are inclined to give to the men who cannot see the truths of Christianity as we see them.

Contrast CHRIST'S TREATMENT of doubt. I have spoken already of His strange partiality for the outsiders—for the scattered heretics up and down the country; of the care with which He loved to deal with them, and of the respect in which He held their intellectual difficulties. Christ never failed to distinguish between doubt and unbelief. Doubt is *"can't believe"*; unbelief is *"won't believe.*" Doubt is honesty; unbelief is obstinacy. Doubt is looking for light; unbelief is content with darkness. Loving darkness rather than light—that is what Christ attacked, and attacked unsparingly. But for the intellectual questioning of Thomas, and Philip, and Nicodemus, and the many others who came to Him to have their great problems solved, He was respectful and generous and tolerant.

And how did He meet their doubts? The Church, as I have said, says, "Brand him!" Christ said, "Teach him." He destroyed by fulfilling. When Thomas came to Him and denied His very resurrection, and stood before Him waiting for the scathing words and lashing for his unbelief, they never came. They never came! Christ gave him facts—facts! No man can go around facts. Christ said, "Behold My hands and My feet." The great god of science at the present time is a fact. It works with facts. Its cry is, "Give me facts. Found anything you like upon facts and we will believe it." The spirit of Christ was the scientific spirit. He founded His religion upon facts; and He asked all men to found their religion upon facts.

Now, get up the facts of Christianity, and take men to the facts. Theologies—and I am not speaking disrespectfully of theology; theology is as scientific a thing as any other science of facts—but theologies are HUMAN VERSIONS of Divine truths, and hence the varieties of the versions and the inconsistencies of them. I would allow a man to select whichever version of this truth he liked *afterwards*; but I would ask him to begin with no version, but go back to the facts and base his Christian life upon these.

That is the great lesson of the New Testament way of looking at doubt—of Christ's treatment of doubt. It is not "Brand him!"—but lovingly, wisely and tenderly to teach him. Faith is never opposed to reason in the New Testament; it is opposed to sight. You will find that a principle worth thinking over. *Faith is never opposed to reason in the New Testament, but to sight.*

With these principles in mind as to the origin of doubt, and as to Christ's treatment of it, how are we ourselves to deal with those who are in intellectual difficulty?

In the first place, I think *we must make all the concessions to them that we conscientiously can.*

When a doubter first encounters you, he pours out a deluge of abuse of churches, and ministers, and creeds, and Christians. Nine-tenths of what he says is probably true. Make concessions. Agree with him. It does him good to unburden himself of these things. He has been cherishing them for years—laying them up against Christians, against the Church, and against Christianity; and now he is startled to find the first Christian with whom he has talked over the thing almost entirely agrees with him. We are, of course, not responsible for everything that is said in the name of Christianity; but a man does not give up medicine because there are quack doctors, and no man has a right to give up his Christianity because there are spurious or inconsistent Christians. Then, as I already said, creeds are human versions of Divine truths; and we do not ask a man to accept all the creeds, any more than we ask him to accept all the Christians. We ask him to accept Christ, and the facts about Christ and the words of Christ. You will find the battle is half won when you have endorsed the man's objections, and possibly added a great many more to the charges which he has against ourselves. These men are IN REVOLT against the kind of religion which we exhibit to the world—against the cant that is taught in the name of Christianity. And if the men that have never seen the real thing—if you could show them that, they would receive it as eagerly as you do. They are merely in revolt against the imperfections and inconsistencies of those who represent Christ to the world.

Second: *Beg them to set aside, by an act of will, all unsolved problems*: such as the problem of the origin of evil, the problem of the Trinity, the problem of the relation of human will and predestination, and so on—problems which have been investigated for thousands of years without result—ask them to set those problems aside as insoluble. In the meantime, just as a man who is studying mathematics may be asked to set aside the problem of squaring the circle, let him go on with what can be done, and what has been done, and leave out of sight the impossible.

You will find that will relieve the skeptic's mind of a great deal of UNNECESSARY CARGO that has been in his way.

Thirdly: *Talking about difficulties, as a rule, only aggravates them.*

Entire satisfaction to the intellect is unattainable about any of the greater problems, and if you try to get to the bottom of them by argument, there is no bottom there; and therefore you make the matter worse. But I would say what is known, and what can be honestly and philosophically and scientifically said about one or two of the difficulties that the doubter raises, just to show him that you can do it—to show him that you are not a fool—that you are not merely groping in the dark yourself, but you have found whatever basis is possible. But I would not go around all the doctrines. I would simply do that with one or two; because the moment you cut off one, a hundred other heads will grow in its place. It would be a pity if all these problems could be solved. The joy of the intellectual life would be largely gone. I would not rob a man of his problems, nor would I have another man rob me of my problems. They are the delight of life, and the whole intellectual world would be stale and unprofitable if we knew everything.

Fourthly—and this is the great point: *Turn away from the reason and go into the man's moral life.*

I don't mean, go into his moral life and see if the man is living in conscious sin, which is the great blinder of the eyes—I am speaking now of honest doubt; but open a new door into THE PRACTICAL SIDE OF MAN'S NATURE.

Entreat him not to postpone life and his life's usefulness until he has settled the problems of the universe. Tell him those problems will never all be settled; that his life will be done before he has begun to settle them; and ask him what he is doing with his life meantime. Charge him with wasting his life and his usefulness; and invite him to deal with the moral and practical difficulties of the world, and leave the intellectual difficulties as he goes along. To spend time upon these is proving the less important before the more important; and, as the French say, "The good is the enemy of the best." It is a good thing to think; it is a better thing to work—it is a better thing to do good. And you have him there, you see. He can't get beyond that. You have to tell him, in fact, that there are two organs of knowledge: the one reason, the other obedience. And now tell him, as he has tried the first and found the little in it, just for a moment or two to join you in trying the second. And when he asks whom he is to obey, you tell him there is but One, and lead him to the great historical figure who calls all men to Him: the one perfect life—the one Savior of mankind—the one Light of the world. Ask him to begin to OBEY CHRIST; and, doing His will, he shall know of the doctrine whether it be of God.

That, I think, is about the only thing you can do with a man: to get him into practical contact with the needs of the world, and to let him lose his intellectual difficulties meantime. Don't ask him to give them up altogether. Tell him to solve them afterward one by one if he can, but meantime to give his life to Christ and his time to the kingdom of God. You fetch him completely around when you do that. You have taken him away from the false side of his nature, and to the practical and moral side of his nature; and for the first time in his life, perhaps, he puts things in their true place. He puts his nature in the relations in which it ought to be, and he then only begins to live. And by obedience he will soon become a learner and pupil for himself, and Christ will teach him things, and he will find whatever problems are solvable gradually solved as he goes along the path of practical duty.

Now, let me, in closing, give an instance of how to deal with specific points.

The question of miracles is thrown at my head every second day:

"What do you say to a man when he says to you, 'Why do you believe in miracles?'"

I say, "Because I have seen them."

He asks, "When?"

I say, "Yesterday."

"Where?"

"Down such-and-such a street I saw a man who was a drunkard redeemed by the power of an unseen Christ and saved from sin. That is a miracle."

The best apologetic for Christianity is a Christian. That is a fact which the man cannot get over. There are fifty other arguments for miracles, but none so good as that you have seen them. Perhaps you are one yourself. But take a man and show him a miracle with his own eyes. Then he will believe.

The Programme
of Christianity

W hat does God do all day?" once asked
a little boy. One could wish that more
grown-up people would ask so very real a question. Unfortunately, most of us are not even boys
in religious intelligence, but only very unthink-
ing children. It no more occurs to us that God
is engaged in any particular work in the world
than it occurs to a little child that its father does
anything except be its father. Its father may be a
Cabinet Minister absorbed in the nation's work, or
an inventor deep in schemes for the world's good;
but to this master-egoist he is father, and nothing
more. Childhood, whether in the physical or moral

world, is the great self-centered period of life; and a personal God who satisfies personal ends is all that for a long time many a Christian understands.

But as clearly as there comes to the growing child a knowledge of its father's part in the world, and a sense of what real life means, there must come to every Christian whose growth is true some richer sense of the meaning of Christianity and a larger view of Christ's purpose for mankind. To miss this is to miss the whole splendour and glory of Christ's religion. Next to losing the sense of a personal Christ, the worst evil that can befall a Christian is to have no sense of anything else. To grow up in complacent belief that God has no business in this great groaning world of human beings except to attend to a few saved souls is the negation of all religion. The first great epoch in a Christian's life, after the awe and wonder of its dawn, is when there breaks into his mind some sense that Christ has a purpose for mankind, a purpose beyond him and his needs, beyond the churches and their creeds, beyond Heaven and its saints—a purpose which embraces every man and woman born, every kindred and nation formed, which regards not their spiritual good alone but their welfare in every part, their progress, their health, their work, their wages, their happiness in this present world.

What, then, does Christ do all day? By what further conception shall we augment the selfish view of why Christ lived and died?

I shall mislead no one, I hope, if I say—for I wish to put the social side of Christianity in its strongest light—that Christ did not come into the world to give men religion. He never mentioned the word religion. Religion was in the world before Christ came, and it lives to-day in a million souls who have never heard His name. *What God does all day* is not to sit waiting in churches for people to come and worship Him. It is true that God is in churches and in all kinds of churches, and is found by many in churches more immediately than anywhere else. It is also true that while Christ did not give men religion He gave a new direction to the religious aspiration bursting forth then and now and always from the whole world's heart. But it was His purpose to enlist these aspirations on behalf of some definite practical good. The religious people of those days did nothing with their religion except attend to its observances. Even the priest, after he had been to the temple, thought his work was done; when he met the wounded man he passed by on the other side. Christ reversed all this—tried to reverse it, for He is only now beginning to succeed. The tendency of the religions of all time has been to care more for religion than for humanity; Christ cared more for humanity than for religion—rather His care for humanity was the chief expression of His religion. He was not indifferent to observances, but the practices of the people bulked in His thoughts before the practices of the Church. It has been pointed out as a blemish on the immortal allegory of Bunyan that the Pilgrim never *did* anything, anything but save his soul. The remark is scarcely fair, for the allegory is designedly the story of a soul in a single relation; and besides, he did do a little. But the warning may well be weighed. The Pilgrim's one thought, his work by day, his dream by night, was *escape*. He took little part in the world through which he passed. He was a *Pilgrim* travelling through it; his business was to get through safe. Whatever this is, it is not Christianity. Christ's conception of Christianity was heavens removed from that of a man setting out from the City of Destruction to save his soul. It was rather that of a man dwelling amidst the Destructions of the City and planning escapes for the souls of others—escapes not to the other world, but to purity and peace and righteousness in this. In reality Christ never said "Save your soul." It is a mistranslation which says that. What He said was, "Save your life." And this not because the first is nothing, but only because it is so very great a thing that only the second can accomplish it. But the new word altruism—the translation of "love thy neighbour as thyself"—is slowly finding its way into current Christian speech. The People's Progress, not less than the Pilgrim's Progress, is daily becoming a graver concern to the Church. A popular theology with unselfishness as part at least of its root, a theology which appeals no longer to fear, but to the generous heart in man, has already dawned, and more clearly than ever men are beginning to see what Christ really came into this world to do.

What Christ came here for was to make a better world. The world in which we live is an unfinished world. It is not wise, it is not happy, it is not pure, it is not good—it is not even sanitary. Humanity is little more than raw material. Almost everything has yet to be done to it. Before the days of Geology people thought the earth was finished. It is by no means finished. The work of Creation is going on. Before the spectroscope, men thought the universe was finished. We know now it is just beginning. And this teeming universe of men in which we live has almost all its finer colour and beauty yet to take. Christ came to complete it. The fires of its passions were not yet cool; their heat had to be transformed into finer energies. The ideals for its future were all to shape, the forces to realize them were not yet born. The poison of its sins had met no antidote, the gloom of its doubt no light, the weight of its sorrow no rest. These the Saviour of the world, the Light of men, would do and be. This, roughly, was His scheme.

Now this was a prodigious task—to recreate the world. How was it to be done? God's way of making worlds is to make them make themselves. When He made the earth He made a rough ball of matter and supplied it with a multitude of tools to mould it into form—the rain-drop to carve it, the glacier to smooth it, the river to nourish it, the flower to adorn it. God works always with agents, and this is our way when we want any great thing done, and this was Christ's way when He undertook the finishing of Humanity. He had a vast intractable mass of matter to deal with, and He required a multitude of tools. Christ's tools were men. Hence His first business in the world was to make a collection of men. In other words He founded a Society.

THE FOUNDING OF THE SOCIETY

It is a somewhat startling thought—it will not be misunderstood—that Christ probably did not save many people while He was here. Many an evangelist, in that direction, has done much more. He never intended to finish the world single-handed, but announced from the first that others would not only take part, but do "greater things" than He. For amazing as was the attention He was able to give to individuals, this was not the whole aim He had in view. His immediate work was to enlist men in His enterprise, to rally them into a great company or Society for the carrying out of His plans.

The name by which this Society was known was *The Kingdom of God*. Christ did not coin this name; it was an old expression, and good men had always hoped and prayed that some such Society would be born in their midst. But it was never either defined or set agoing in earnest until Christ made its realization the passion of His life.

How keenly He felt regarding His task, how enthusiastically He set about it, every page of His life bears witness. All reformers have one or two great words which they use incessantly, and by mere reiteration imbed indelibly in the thought and history of their time. Christ's great word was the Kingdom of God. Of all the words of His that have come down to us this is by far the commonest. One hundred times it occurs in the Gospels. When He preached He had almost always this for a text. His sermons were explanations of the aims of His Society, of the different things it was like, of whom its membership consisted, what they were to do or to be, or not do or not be. And even when

He does not actually use the word, it is easy to see that all He said and did had reference to this. Philosophers talk about thinking in categories— the mind living, as it were, in a particular room with its own special furniture, pictures, and view-points, these giving a consistent direction and colour to all that is there thought or expressed. It was in the category of the Kingdom that Christ's thought moved. Though one time He said He came to save the lost, or at another time to give men life, or to do His Father's will, these were all included among the objects of His Society.

No one can ever know what Christianity is till he has grasped this leading thought in the mind of Christ. Peter and Paul have many wonderful and necessary things to tell us about what Christ was and did; but we are looking now at what Christ's own thought was. Do not think this is a mere modern theory. These are His own life-plans taken from His own lips. Do not allow any isolated text, even though it seem to sum up for you the Christian life, to keep you from trying to understand Christ's Programme as a whole. The perspective of Christ's teaching is not everything, but without it everything will be distorted and untrue. There is much good in a verse, but often much evil. To see some small soul pirouetting throughout life on a single text, and judging all the world because it cannot find a partner, is not a Christian sight. Christianity does not grudge such souls their comfort. What it grudges is that they make Christ's Kingdom uninhabitable to thoughtful minds. Be sure that whenever the religion of Christ appears small, or forbidding, or narrow, or inhuman, you are dealing not with the whole—which is a matchless moral symmetry—nor even with an arch or column—for every detail is perfect—but with some cold stone removed from its place and suggesting nothing of the glorious structure from which it came.

Tens of thousands of persons who are familiar with religious truths have not noticed yet that Christ ever founded a Society at all. The reason is partly that people have read texts instead of reading their Bible, partly that they have studied Theology instead of studying Christianity, and partly because of the noiselessness and invisibility of the Kingdom of God itself. Nothing truer was ever said of this Kingdom than that "It cometh without observation." Its first discovery, therefore, comes to the Christian with all the force of a revelation. The sense of belonging to such a Society transforms life. It is the difference between being a solitary knight tilting single-handed, and often defeated, at whatever enemy one chances to meet on one's little acre of life, and the *feel* of belonging to a mighty army marching throughout all time to a certain victory. This note of universality given to even the humblest work we do, this sense of comradeship, this link with history, this thought of a definite campaign, this promise of success, is the possession of every obscurest unit in the Kingdom of God.

THE PROGRAMME OF THE SOCIETY

Hundreds of years before Christ's Society was formed, its Programme had been issued to the world. I cannot think of any scene in history more dramatic than when Jesus entered the church in Nazareth and read it to the people. Not that when He appropriated to Himself that venerable fragment from Isaiah He was uttering a manifesto or announcing His formal Programme. Christ never did things formally. We think of the words, as He probably thought of them, not in their old-world historical significance, nor as a full expression of His future aims, but as a summary of great moral facts now and always to be realized in the world since he appeared.

Remember as you read the words to what grim reality they refer. Recall what Christ's problem really was, what His Society was founded for. This Programme deals with a real world. Think of it as you read—not of the surface-world, but of the world as it is, as it sins and weeps, and curses and suffers and sends up its long cry to God. Limit it if you like to the world around your door, but think of it—of the city and the hospital and the dungeon and the graveyard, of the sweating-shop and the pawn-shop and the drink-shop; think of the cold, the cruelty, the fever, the famine, the ugliness, the loneliness, the pain. And then try to keep down the lump in your throat as you take up His Programme and read—

> TO BIND UP THE BROKEN-HEARTED:
> TO PROCLAIM LIBERTY TO THE CAPTIVES:
> TO COMFORT ALL THAT MOURN:
> TO GIVE UNTO THEM—
>   BEAUTY FOR ASHES,
>   THE OIL OF JOY FOR MOURNING,
>   THE GARMENT OF PRAISE FOR THE
>   SPIRIT OF HEAVINESS.

What an exchange—Beauty for Ashes, Joy for Mourning, Liberty for Chains! No marvel "the eyes of all them that were in the synagogue were fastened on Him" as He read; or that they "wondered at the gracious words which proceeded out of His lips." Only one man in that congregation, only one man in the world to-day could hear these accents with dismay—the man, the culprit, who has said hard words of Christ.

We are all familiar with the protest "Of course"—as if there were no other alternative to a person of culture—"Of course I am not a Christian, but I always speak *respectfully* of Christianity." Respectfully of Christianity! No remark fills one's soul with such sadness. One can understand a man as he reads these words being stricken speechless; one can see the soul within him rise to a white heat as each fresh benediction falls upon his ear and drive him, a half-mad enthusiast, to bear them to the world. But in what school has he learned of Christ who offers the Saviour of the world his respect?

Men repudiate Christ's religion because they think it a small and limited thing, a scheme with no large human interests to commend it to this great social age. I ask you to note that there is not one burning interest of the human race which is not represented here. What are the great words of Christianity according to this Programme? Take as specimens these:

LIBERTY,
COMFORT,
BEAUTY,
JOY.

These are among the greatest words of life. Give them their due extension, the significance which Christ undoubtedly saw in them and which Christianity undoubtedly yields, and there is almost no great want or interest of mankind which they do not cover.

These are not only the greatest words of life but they are the best. This Programme, to those who have misread Christianity, is a series of surprises. Observe the most prominent note in it. It is *gladness*. Its first word is "good-tidings," its last is "joy." The saddest words of life are also there—but there as the diseases which Christianity comes to cure. No life that is occupied with such an enterprise could be other than radiant. The contribution of Christianity to the joy of living, perhaps even more to the joy of *thinking*, is unspeakable. The joyful life is the life of the larger mission, the disinterested life, the life of the overflow from self, the "more abundant life" which comes from following Christ. And the joy of thinking is the larger thinking, the thinking of the man who holds in his hand some Programme for Humanity. The Christian is the only man who has any Programme at all—any Programme either for the world or for himself. Goethe, Byron, Carlyle taught Humanity much, but they had no Programme for it. Byron's thinking was suffering; Carlisle's despair. Christianity alone exults. The belief in the universe as moral, the interpretation of history as progress, the faith in good as eternal, in evil as self-consuming, in humanity as evolving—these Christian ideas have transformed the malady of thought into a bounding hope. It was no sentiment but a conviction matured amid calamity and submitted to the tests of life that inspired the great modern poet of optimism to proclaim:—

"Gladness be with thee, Helper of the world!
I think this is the authentic sign and seal
Of Godship, that it ever waxes glad,
And more glad, until gladness blossoms, bursts
Into a rage to suffer for mankind
And recommence at sorrow."

But that is not all. Man's greatest needs are often very homely. And it is almost as much in its fearless recognition of the commonplace woes of life, and its deliberate offerings to minor needs, that the claims of Christianity to be a religion for Humanity stand. Look, for instance, at the closing sentence of this Programme. Who would have expected to find among the special objects of Christ's solicitude the *Spirit of Heaviness?* Supreme needs, many and varied, had been already dealt with on this Programme; many applicants had been met; the list is about to close. Suddenly the writer remembers the nameless malady of the poor—that mysterious disease which the rich share but cannot alleviate, which is too subtle for doctors, too incurable for Parliaments, too unpicturesque for philanthropy, too common even for sympathy. Can Christ meet that?

If Christianity could even deal with the world's Depression, could cure mere dull spirits, it would be the Physician of Humanity. But it can. It has the secret, a hundred secrets, for the lifting of the world's gloom. It cannot immediately remove the physiological causes of dullness—though obedience to its principles can do an infinity to prevent them, and its inspirations can do even more to lift the mind above them. But where the causes are moral or mental or social the remedy is in every Christian's hand. Think of any one at this moment whom the Spirit of Heaviness haunts. You think of a certain old woman. But you know for a fact that you can cure her. You did so, perfectly, only a week ago. A mere visit, and a little present, or the visit without any present, set her up for seven long days, and seven long nights. The machinery of the Kingdom is very simple and very silent, and the most silent parts do most, and we all believe so little in the medicines of Christ that we do not know what ripples of healing are set in motion when we simply smile on one another. Christianity wants nothing so much in the world as sunny people, and the old are hungrier for love than for bread, and the Oil of Joy is very cheap, and if you can help the poor on with a Garment of Praise, it will be better for them than blankets.

Or perhaps you know someone else who is dull—not an old woman this time, but a very rich and important man. But you also know perfectly what makes him dull. It is either his riches or his importance. Christianity can cure either of these though you may not be the person to apply the cure—at a single hearing. Or here is a third case, one of your own servants. It is a case of *monotony*. Prescribe more variety, leisure, recreation—anything to relieve the wearing strain. A fourth case—your most honoured guest: Condition—leisure, health, accomplishments, means; Disease—Spiritual Obesity; Treatment—talent to be put out to usury. And so on down the whole range of life's dejection and *ennui*.

Perhaps you tell me this is not Christianity at all; that everybody could do that. The curious thing is that everybody does not. Good-will to men came into the world with Christ, and wherever that is found, in Christian or heathen land, there Christ is, and there His Spirit works. And if you say that the chief end of Christianity is not the world's happiness, I agree; it was never meant to be; but the strange fact is that, without making it its chief end, it wholly and infallibly, and quite universally, leads to it. Hence the note of Joy, though not the highest on Christ's Programme, is a loud and ringing note, and none who serve in His Society can be long without its music. Time was when a Christian used to apologize for being happy. But the day has always been when he ought to apologize for being miserable.

Christianity, you will observe, really works. And it succeeds not only because it is divine, but because it is so very human—because it is common-sense. Why should the Garment of Praise destroy the Spirit of Heaviness? Because an old woman cannot sing and cry at the same moment. The Society of Christ is a sane Society. Its methods are rational. The principle in the old woman's case is simply that one emotion destroys another. Christianity works, as a railway man would say, with points. It switches souls from valley lines to mountain lines, not stemming the currents of life but diverting them. In the rich man's case the principle of cure is different, but it is again principle, not necromancy. His spirit of heaviness is caused, like any other heaviness, by the earth's attraction. Take away the earth and you take away the attraction. But if Christianity can do anything it can take away the earth. By the wider extension of horizon which it gives, by the new standard of values, by the mere setting of life's small pomps and interests and admirations in the light of the Eternal, it dissipates the world with a breath. All that tends to abolish worldliness tends to abolish unrest, and hence, in the rush of modern life, one far-reaching good of all even commonplace Christian preaching, all Christian literature, all which holds the world doggedly to the idea of a God and a future life, and reminds mankind of Infinity and Eternity.

Side by side with these influences, yet taking the world at a wholly different angle, works another great Christian force. How many opponents of religion are aware that one of the specific objects of Christ's society is Beauty? The charge of vulgarity against Christianity is an old one. If it means that Christianity deals with the ruder elements in human nature, it is true, and that is its glory. But if it means that it has no respect for the finer qualities, the charge is baseless. For Christianity not only encourages whatsoever things are lovely, but wars against that whole theory of life which would exclude them. It prescribes aestheticism. It proscribes asceticism. And for those who preach to Christians that in these enlightened days they must raise the masses by giving them noble sculptures and beautiful paintings and music and public parks, the answer is that these things are all already being given, and given daily, and with an increasing sense of their importance, by the Society of Christ. Take away from the world the beautiful things which have not come from Christ and you will make it poorer scarcely at all. Take away from modern cities the paintings, the monuments, the music for the people, the museums and the parks which are not the gifts of Christian men and Christian municipalities, and in ninety cases out of a hundred you will leave them unbereft of so much as a well-shaped lamp-post.

It is impossible to doubt that the Decorator of the World shall not continue to serve to His later children, and in ever finer forms, the inspirations of beautiful things. More fearlessly than he has ever done, the Christian of modern life will use the noble spiritual leverages of Art. That this world, the people's world, is a bleak and ugly world, we do not forget; it is ever with us. But we esteem too little the mission of beautiful things in haunting the mind with higher thoughts and begetting the mood which leads to God. Physical beauty makes moral beauty. Loveliness does more than destroy ugliness; it destroys matter. A mere touch of it in a room, in a street, even on a door knocker, is a spiritual force. Ask the working-man's wife, and she will tell you there is a moral effect even in a clean table-cloth. If a barrel-organ in a slum can but drown a curse, let no Christian silence it. The mere light and colour of the wall-advertisements are a gift of God to the poor man's sombre world.

One Christmas-time a poor drunkard told me that he had gone out the night before to take his usual chance of the temptations of the street. Close to his door, at a shop window, an angel—so he said—arrested him. It was a large Christmas-card, a glorious white thing with tinsel wings, and as it glittered in the gas-light it flashed into his soul a sudden thought of Heaven. It recalled the earlier heaven of his infancy, and he thought of his mother in the distant glen, and how it would please her if she got this Christmas angel from her prodigal. With money already pledged to the devil he bought the angel, and with it a new soul and future for himself. That was a real angel. For that day as I saw its tinsel pinions shine in his squalid room I knew what Christ's angels were. They are all beautiful things, which daily in common homes are bearing up heavy souls to God.

But do not misunderstand me. This angel was made of pasteboard: a pasteboard angel can never save a soul. Tinsel reflects the sun, but warms nothing. Our Programme must go deeper. Beauty may arrest the drunkard, but it cannot cure him.

It is here that Christianity asserts itself with a supreme individuality. It is here that it parts company with Civilization, with Politics, with all secular schemes of Social Reform. In its diagnosis of human nature it finds that which most other systems ignore; which, if they see, they cannot cure; which, left undestroyed, makes every reform futile, and every inspiration vain. That thing is *Sin*. Christianity, of all other philanthropies, recognizes that man's devouring need is *Liberty*—liberty to stop sinning; to leave the prison of his passions, and shake off the fetters of his past. To surround *Captives* with statues and pictures, to offer *Them-that-are-Bound* a higher wage or a cleaner street or a few more cubic feet of air per head, is solemn trifling. It is a cleaner soul they want; a purer air, or any air at all, for their higher selves.

And where the cleaner soul is to come from apart from Christ I cannot tell. "By no political alchemy," Herbert Spencer tells us, "can you get golden conduct out of leaden instincts." The power to set the heart right, to renew the springs of action, comes from Christ. The sense of the infinite worth of the single soul, and the recoverableness of man at his worst, are the gifts of Christ. The freedom from guilt, the forgiveness of sins, come from Christ's Cross; the hope of immortality springs from Christ's grave. We believe in the gospel of better laws and an improved environment; we hold the religion of Christ to be a social religion; we magnify and call Christian the work of reformers, statesmen, philanthropists, educators, inventors, sanitary officers, and all who directly or remotely aid, abet, or further the higher progress of mankind; but in Him alone, in the fullness of that word, do we see the Saviour of the world.

There are earnest and gifted lives to-day at work among the poor whose lips at least will not name the name of Christ. I speak of them with respect; their shoe-latchets many of us are not worthy to unloose. But because the creed of the neighbouring mission-hall is a travesty of religion they refuse to acknowledge the power of the living Christ to stop man's sin, of the dying Christ to forgive it. O, narrowness of breadth! Because there are ignorant doctors do I yet rail at medicine or start an hospital of my own? Because the poor raw evangelist, or the narrow ecclesiastic, offer their little all to the poor, shall I repudiate all they do not know of Christ because of the little that they do know? Of gospels for the poor which have not some theory, state it how you will, of personal conversion one cannot have much hope. Personal conversion means for life a personal religion, a personal trust in God, a personal debt to Christ, a personal dedication to His cause. These, brought about how you will, are supreme things to aim at, supreme losses if they are missed. Sanctification will come to masses only as it comes to individual men; and to work with Christ's Programme and ignore Christ is to utilize the sun's light without its energy.

But this is not the only point at which the uniqueness of this Society appears. There is yet another depth in humanity which no other system even attempts to sound. We live in a world not only of sin but of sorrow—

> *"There is no flock, however watched*
>   *and tended,*
> *But one dead lamb is there;*
> *There is no home, howe'er defended,*
> *But has one vacant chair."*

When the flock thins, and the chair empties, who is to be near to heal? At that moment the gospels of the world are on trial. In the presence of death how will they act? Act! They are blotted out of existence. Philosophy, Politics, Reforms, are no more. The Picture Galleries close. The sculptures hide. The Committees disperse. There is crape on the door; the world withdraws. Observe, *it withdraws.* It has no mission.

So awful in its loneliness was this hour that the Romans paid a professional class; to step in with its mummeries and try to fill it. But that is Christ's own hour. Next to Righteousness the greatest word of Christianity is Comfort. Christianity has almost a monopoly of Comfort Renan was never nearer the mark than when he spoke of the Bible as "the great Book of the Consolation of Humanity." Christ's Programme is full of Comfort, studded with Comfort: "to bind up the Broken-Hearted, to Comfort all that mourn, to Give unto them that mourn in Zion." Even the "good tidings" to the "meek" are, in the Hebrew, a message to the "afflicted" or "the poor." The word Gospel itself comes down through the Greek from this very passage, so that whatever else Christ's Gospel means it is first an Evangel for suffering men.

One note in this Programme jars with all the rest. When Christ read from Isaiah that day He never finished the passage. A terrible word, Vengeance, yawned like a precipice across His path; and in the middle of a sentence "He closed the Book, and gave it again to the minister, and sat down." A Day of Vengeance from our God—these were the words before which Christ paused. When the prophet proclaimed it some great historical fulfilment was in his mind. Had the people to whom Christ read been able to understand its ethical equivalents He would probably have read on. For, so understood, instead of filling the mind with fear, the thought of this dread Day inspires it with a solemn gratitude. The work of the Avenger is a necessity. It is part of God's philanthropy.

For I have but touched the surface in speaking of the sorrow of the world as if it came from people dying. It comes from people living. Before ever the Broken-Hearted can be healed a hundred greater causes of suffering than death must be destroyed. Before the Captive can be free a vaster prison than his own sins must be demolished. There are hells on earth into which no breath of heaven can ever come; these must be swept away. There are social soils in which only unrighteousness can flourish; these must be broken up.

And that is the work of the Day of Vengeance. When is that day? It is now. Who is the Avenger? Law. What Law? Criminal Law, Sanitary Law, Social Law, Natural Law. Wherever the poor are trodden upon or tread upon one another; wherever the air is poison and the water foul; wherever want stares, and vice reigns, and rags rot—there the Avenger takes his stand. Whatever makes it more difficult for the drunkard to reform, for the children to be pure, for the widow to earn a wage, for any of the wheels of progress to revolve—with these he deals. Delay him not. He is the messenger of Christ. Despair of him not, distrust him not. His Day dawns slowly, but his work is sure. Though evil stalks the world, it is on the way to execution; though wrong reigns, it must end in self-combustion. The very nature of things is God's Avenger; the very story of civilization is the history of Christ's Throne.

Anything that prepares the way for a better social state is the fit work of the followers of Christ. Those who work on the more spiritual levels leave too much unhonoured the slow toil of multitudes of unchurched souls who prepare the material or moral environments without which these higher labours are in vain. Prevention is Christian as well as cure; and Christianity travels sometimes by the most circuitous paths. It is given to some to work for immediate results, and from year to year they are privileged to reckon up a balance of success. But these are not always the greatest in the Kingdom of God. The men who get no stimulus from any visible reward, whose lives pass while the objects for which they toil are still too far away to comfort them; the men who hold aloof from dazzling schemes and earn the misunderstanding of the crowd because they foresee remoter issues, who even oppose a seeming good because a deeper evil lurks beyond—these are the statesmen of the Kingdom of God.

THE MACHINERY OF THE SOCIETY

Such in dimmest outline is the Programme of Christ's Society. Did you know that all this was going on in the world? Did you know that Christianity was such a living and purpose-like thing? Look back to the day when that Programme was given, and you will see that it was not merely written on paper. Watch the drama of the moral order rise up, scene after scene, in history. Study the social evolution of humanity, the spread of righteousness, the amelioration of life, the freeing of slaves, the elevation of woman, the purification of religion, and ask what these can be if not the coming of the Kingdom of God on earth. For it is precisely through the movements of nations and the lives of men that this Kingdom comes. Christ might have done all this work Himself, with His own hands. But He did not. The crowning wonder of His scheme is that He entrusted it to men. It is the supreme glory of humanity that the machinery for its redemption should have been placed within itself. I think the saddest thing in Christ's life was that after founding a Society with aims so glorious He had to go away and leave it.

But in reality He did not leave it. The old theory that God made the world, made it as an inventor would make a machine, and then stood looking on to see it work, has passed away. God is no longer a remote spectator of the natural world, but imma-nent in it, pervading matter by His present Spirit, and ordering it by His Will. So Christ is immanent in men. His work is to move the hearts and inspire the lives of men, and through such hearts to move and reach the world. Men, only men, can carry out this work. This humanness, this inwardness, of the Kingdom is one reason why some scarcely see that it exists at all. We measure great move-ments by the loudness of their advertisement, or the place their externals fill in the public eye. This Kingdom has no externals. The usual methods of propagating a great cause were entirely discarded by Christ. The sword He declined; money He had none; literature He never used; the Church dis-owned Him; the State crucified Him. Planting His ideals in the hearts of a few poor men, He started them out unheralded to revolutionize the world. They did it by making friends and by making ene-mies; they went about, did good, sowed seed, died, and lived again in the lives of those they helped. These in turn, a fraction of them, did the same. They met, they prayed, they talked of Christ, they loved, they went among other men, and by act and word passed on their secret. The machinery of the Kingdom of God is purely social. It acts, not by commandment, but by contagion; not by fiat, but by friendship. "The Kingdom of God is like unto leaven, which a woman took and hid in three measures of meal till the whole was leavened."

After all, like all great discoveries once they are made, this seems absolutely the most feasible method that could have been devised. Men *must* live among men. Men *must* influence men. Organizations, institutions, churches, have too much rigidity for a thing that is to flood the world. The only fluid in the world is man. War might have won for Christ's cause a passing victory; wealth might have purchased a superficial triumph; political power might have gained a temporary success. But in these, there is no note of universality, of solidarity, of immortality. To live through the centuries and pervade the uttermost ends of the earth, to stand while kingdoms tottered and civilizations changed, to survive fallen churches and crumbling creeds—there was no soil for the Kingdom of God like the hearts of common men. Some who have written about this Kingdom have emphasized its moral grandeur, others its universality, others its adaptation to man's needs. One great writer speaks of its prodigious originality, another chiefly notices its success. I confess what almost strikes me most is the miracle of its simplicity.

Men, then, are the only means God's Spirit has of accomplishing His purpose. What men? You.

Is it worth doing, or is it not? Is it worth while joining Christ's Society or is it not? What do *you* do all day? What is your personal stake in the coming of the Kingdom of Christ on earth? You are not interested in religion, you tell me; you do not care for your "soul." It was not about your religion I ventured to ask, still less about your soul. That you have no religion, that you do not care for your soul, does not absolve you from caring for the world in which you live. But you do not believe in this church, you reply, or accept this doctrine, or that. Christ does not, in the first instance, ask your thoughts, but your work. No man has a right to postpone his *life* for the sake of his thoughts. Why? Because this is a real world, not a *think* world. Treat it as a real world—act. Think by all means, but think also of what is actual, of what like the stern world is, of low much even you, creedless and churchless, could do to make it better. The thing to be anxious about is not to be right with man, but with mankind. And, so far as I know, there is nothing so on all fours with mankind as Christianity.

There are versions of Christianity, it is true, which no self-respecting mind can do other than disown—versions so hard, so narrow, so unreal, so super-theological, that practical men can find in them neither outlet for their lives nor resting-place for their thoughts. With these we have nothing to do. With these Christ had nothing to do—except to oppose them with every word and act of His life. It too seldom occurs to those who repudiate Christianity because of its narrowness or its unpracticalness, its sanctimoniousness or its dullness, that these were the very things which Christ strove against and unweariedly condemned. It was the one risk of His religion being given to the common people—an inevitable risk which He took without reserve—that its infinite lustre should be tarnished in the fingering of the crowd or have its great truths narrowed into mean and unworthy moulds as they passed from lip to lip. But though the crowd is the object of Christianity, it is not its custodian. Deal with the Founder of this great Commonwealth Himself. Any man of honest purpose who will take the trouble to inquire at first hand what Christianity really is, will find it a thing he cannot get away from. Without either argument or pressure, by the mere practicalness of its aims and the pathos of its compassions, it forces its august claim upon every serious life.

He who joins this Society finds himself in a large place. The Kingdom of God is a Society of the best men, working for the best ends, according to the best methods. Its membership is a multitude whom no man can number; its methods are as various as human nature; its field is the world. It is a Commonwealth, yet it honours a King; it is a Social Brotherhood, but it acknowledges the Fatherhood of God. Though not a Philosophy the world turns to it for light; though not Political it is the incubator of all great laws. It is more human than the State, for it deals with deeper needs; more Catholic than the Church, for it includes whom the Church rejects. It is a Propaganda, yet it works not by agitation but by ideals. It is a Religion, yet it holds the worship of God to be mainly the service of man. Though not a Scientific Society its watch-word is Evolution; though not an Ethic it possesses the Sermon on the Mount. This mysterious Society owns no wealth but distributes fortunes. It has no minutes for history keeps them; no member's roll for no one could make it. Its entry-money is nothing; its subscription, all you have The Society never meets and it never adjourns. Its law is one word—loyalty; its Gospel one message—love. Verily "Whosoever will lose his life for My sake shall find it."

The Programme for the other life is not out yet. For this world, for these faculties, for his one short life, I know nothing that is offered to man to compare with membership in the Kingdom of God. Among the mysteries which compass the world beyond, none is greater than how there can be in store for man a work more wonderful, a life more God-like than this. If you know anything better, live for it; if not, in the name of God and of Humanity, carry out Christ's plan.

The City Without a Church

I SAW THE CITY

Two very startling things arrest us in John's vision of the future. The first is that the likest thing to Heaven he could think of was a City; the second, that there was no Church in that City.

Almost nothing more revolutionary could be said, even to the modern world, in the name of religion. *No Church*—that is the defiance of religion; a *City*—that is the antipodes of Heaven. Yet John combines these contradictions in one daring image, and holds up to the world the picture of a City without a Church as his ideal of the heavenly life.

By far the most original thing here is the simple conception of Heaven as a City. The idea of religion without a Church—"I saw no Temple therein"—is anomalous enough; but the association of the blessed life with a City—the one place in the world from which Heaven seems most far away—is something wholly new in religious thought. No other religion which has a Heaven ever had a Heaven like this. The Greek, if he looked forward at all, awaited the Elysian Fields; the Eastern sought Nirvana. All other Heavens have been Gardens, Dreamlands—passivities more or less aimless. Even to the majority among ourselves Heaven is a siesta and not a City. It remained for John to go straight to the other extreme and select the citadel of the world's fever, the ganglion of its unrest, the heart and focus of its most strenuous toil, as the framework for his ideal of the blessed life.

The Heaven of Christianity is different from all other Heavens, because the religion of Christianity is different from all other religions. Christianity is the religion of Cities. It moves among real things. Its sphere is the street, the market-place, the working-life of the world.

And what interests one for the present in John's vision is not so much what it reveals of a Heaven beyond, but what it suggests of the nature of the heavenly life in this present world. Find

out what a man's Heaven is—no matter whether
it be a dream or a reality, no matter whether it
refer to an actual Heaven or to a Kingdom of God
to be realized on earth—and you pass by an easy
discovery to what his religion is; And herein lies
one value at least of this allegory. It is a touchstone
for Christianity, a test for the solidity or the insi-
pidity of one's religion, for the wholesomeness or
the fatuousness of one's faith, for the usefulness or
the futility of one's life. For this vision of the City
marks off in lines which no eye can mistake the
true area which the religion of Christ is meant to
inhabit, and announces for all time the real nature
of the saintly life.

City life is human life at its intensest, man in
his most real relations. And the nearer one draws
to reality, the nearer one draws to the working
sphere of religion. Wherever real life is, there
Christ goes. And He goes there, not only because
the great need lies there, but because there is
found, so to speak, the raw material with which
Christianity works—the life of man. To do something with this, to infuse something into this, to
save and inspire and sanctify this, the actual working life of the world, is what He came for. Without human life to act upon, without the relations
of men with one another, of master with servant,
husband with wife, buyer with seller, creditor

with debtor, there is no such thing as Christianity. With actual things, with Humanity in its everyday dress, with the traffic of the streets, with gates and houses, with work and wages, with sin and poverty, with these *things*, and all the things and all the relations and all the people of the City, Christianity has to do and has more to do than with anything else. To conceive of the Christian religion as itself a thing—a something which can exist apart from life; to think of it as something added on to being, something kept in a separate compartment called the soul, as an extra accomplishment like music, or a special talent like art, is totally to misapprehend its nature. It is that which fills all compartments. It is that which makes the whole life music and every separate action a work of art. Take away action and it is not. Take away people, houses, streets, character, and it ceases to be. Without these there may be sentiment, or rapture, or adoration, or superstition; there may even be religion, but there can never be the religion of the Son of Man.

If Heaven were a siesta, religion might be conceived of as a reverie. If the future life were to be mainly spent in a Temple, the present life might be mainly spent in Church. But if Heaven be a City, the life of those who are going there must be a real life. The man who would enter John's Heaven, no matter what piety or what faith he may profess, must be a real man. Christ's gift to men was life, a rich and abundant life. And life is meant for living. An abundant life does not show itself in abundant dreaming, but in abundant living—in abundant living among real and tangible objects and to actual and practical purposes. "His servants," John tells us, "shall serve." In this vision of the City he confronts us with a new definition of a Christian man—the perfect saint is the perfect citizen.

To make Cities—that is what we are here for. To make good Cities—that is for the present hour the main work of Christianity. For the City is strategic. It makes the towns: the towns make the villages; the villages make the country. He who makes the City makes the world. After all, though men make Cities, it is Cities which make men. Whether our national life is great or mean, whether our social virtues are mature or stunted, whether our sons are moral or vicious, whether religion is possible or impossible, depends upon the City. When Christianity shall take upon itself in full responsibility the burden and care of Cities the Kingdom of God will openly come on earth. What Christianity waits for also, as its final apologetic and justification to the world, is the founding of a City which shall be in visible reality a City of God. People do not dispute that religion is in the

Church. What is now wanted is to let them see it in the City. One Christian City, one City in any part of the earth, whose citizens from the greatest to the humblest lived in the spirit of Christ, where religion had overflowed the Churches and passed into the streets, inundating every house and work-shop, and permeating the whole social and com-mercial life—one such Christian City would seal the redemption of the world.

Some such City, surely, was what John saw in his dream. Whatever reference we may find there to a world to come, is it not equally lawful to seek the scene upon this present world? John saw his City *descending out of Heaven*. It was, moreover, no strange apparition, but a City which he knew. It was Jerusalem, a new *Jerusalem*. The signifi-cance of that name has been altered for most of us by religious poetry; we spell it with a capital and speak of the New Jerusalem as a synonym for Heaven. Yet why not take it simply as it stands, as a new Jerusalem? Try to restore the natural force of the expression—suppose John to have lived to-day and to have said London? "I saw a new London?" Jerusalem was John's London. All the grave and sad suggestion that the word London brings up to-day to the modern reformer, the word Jerusalem recalled to him. What in his deepest hours he longed and prayed for was a new Jerusalem, a reformed Jerusalem. And just as it is given to the man in modern England who is a prophet, to the man who believes in God and in the moral order of the world, to discern a new London shaping itself through all the sin and chaos of the City, so was it given to John to see a new Jerusalem rise from the ruins of the old.

We have no concern—it were contrary to critical method—to press the allegory in detail. What we take from it, looked at in this light, is the broad conception of a transformed City, the great Christian thought that the very Cities where we live, with all their suffering and sin, shall one day, by the gradual action of the forces of Christianity, be turned into Heavens on earth. This is a spectacle which profoundly concerns the world. To the reformer, the philanthropist, the economist, the politician, this Vision of the City is the great classic of social literature. What John saw, we may fairly take it, was the future of all Cities. It was the dawn of a new social order, a regenerate humanity, a purified society, an actual transformation of the Cities of the world into Cities of God.

This City, then, which John saw is none other than your City, the place where you live—as it might be, and as you are to help to make it. It is London, Berlin, New York, Paris, Melbourne, Calcutta—these as they might be, and in some infinitesimal degree as they have already begun to be. In each of these, and in every City throughout the world to-day, there is a City descending out of Heaven from God. Each one of us is daily building up this City or helping to keep it back. Its walls rise slowly, but, as we believe in God, the building can never cease. For the might of those who build, be they few or many, is so surely greater than the might of those who retard, that no day's sun sets over any City in the land that does not see some stone of the invisible City laid. To believe this is faith. To live for this is Christianity.

The project is delirious? Yes—to atheism. To John it was the most obvious thing in the world. Nay, knowing all he knew, its realization was inevitable. We forget, when the thing strikes us as strange, that John knew Christ. Christ was the Light of the *World*—the Light of the World. This is all that he meant by his Vision, that Christ is the Light of the World. This Light, John saw, would fall everywhere—especially upon Cities. It was irresistible and inextinguishable. No darkness could stand before it. One by one the Cities of the world would give up their night. Room by room, house by house, street by street, they would be changed. Whatsoever worketh abomination or maketh a lie would disappear. Sin, pain, sorrow, would silently pass away. One day the walls of the City would be jasper; the very streets would be paved with gold. Then the kings of the earth would bring their glory and honour into it. In the midst of the streets there should be a tree of Life. And its leaves would go forth for the healing of the nations.

Survey the Cities of the world today, survey your own City—town, village, home—and prophesy. God's kingdom is surely to come in this world. God's will is surely to be done on earth as it is done in Heaven. Is not this one practicable way of realizing it? When a prophet speaks of something that is to be, that coming event is usually brought about by no unrelated cause or sudden shock, but in the ordered course of the world's drama. With Christianity as the supreme actor in the world's drama, the future of its Cities is even now quite clear. Project the lines of Christian and social progress to their still far off goal, and see even now that Heaven must come to earth.

HIS SERVANTS SHALL SERVE

If any one wishes to know what he can do to help on the work of God in the world let him make a City, or a street, or a house of a City. Men complain of the indefiniteness of religion. There are thousands ready in their humble measure to offer some personal service for the good of men, but they do not know where to begin. Let me tell you where to begin—where Christ told His disciples to begin, at the nearest City. I promise you that before one week's work is over you will never again be haunted by the problem of the indefiniteness of Christianity. You will see so much to do, so many actual things to be set right, so many merely material conditions to alter, so much striving with employers of labour, and City councils, and trade agitators, and Boards, and Vestries, and Committees; so much pure unrelieved uninspiring hard work, that you will begin to wonder whether in all this naked realism you are on holy ground at all. Do not be afraid of missing Heaven in seeking a better earth. The distinction between secular and sacred is a confusion and not a contrast; and it is only because the secular is so intensely sacred that so many eyes are blind before it. The really secular thing in life is the spirit which despises under that name what is but part of the everywhere present work and will of God. Be sure that, down to the last and pettiest detail, all that concerns a better world is the direct concern of Christ.

I make this, then, in all seriousness as a definite practical proposal. You wish, you say, to be a religious man. Well, be one. There is your City; begin. But what are you to believe? Believe in your City.

What else? In Jesus Christ. What about Him? That He wants to make your City better; that that is what He would be doing if He lived there. What else? Believe in yourself—that you, even you, can do some of the work which He would like done, and that unless you do it, it will remain undone. How are you to begin? As Christ did. First He looked at the City; then He wept over it; then He died for it.

Where are you to begin? Begin where you are. Make that one corner, room, house, office as like Heaven as you can. Begin? Begin with the paper on the walls, make that beautiful; with the air, keep it fresh; with the very drains, make them sweet; with the furniture, see that it be honest. Abolish whatsoever worketh abomination—in food, in drink, in luxury, in books, in art; whatsoever maketh a lie—in conversation, in social intercourse, in correspondence, in domestic life. This done, you have arranged for a Heaven, but you have not got it. Heaven lies within, in kindness, in humbleness, in unselfishness, in faith, in love, in service. To get these in, get Christ in. Teach all in the house about Christ—what He did, and what He said, and how He lived, and how He died, and how He dwells in them, and how He makes all one. Teach it not as a doctrine, but as a discovery, as your own discovery. Live your own discovery.

Then pass out into the City. Do all to it that you have done at home. Beautify it, ventilate it, drain it. Let nothing enter it that can defile the streets, the stage, the newspaper offices, the book-sellers' counters; nothing that maketh a lie in its warehouses, its manufactures, its shops, its art galleries, its advertisements. Educate it, amuse it, church it. Christianize capital; dignify labour. Join Councils and Committees. Provide for the poor, the sick, and the widow. So will you serve the City.

If you ask me which of all these things is the most important, I reply that among them there is only one thing of superlative importance and that is *yourself.* By far the greatest thing a man can do for his City is to be a good man. Simply to live there as a good man, as a Christian man of action and practical citizen, is the first and highest con-tribution any one can make to its salvation. Let a City be a Sodom or a Gomorrah, and if there be but ten righteous men in it, it will be saved.

It is here that the older, the more individual, conception of Christianity, did such mighty work for the world—it produced good men. It is good-ness that tells, goodness first and goodness last. Good men even with small views are immeasur-ably more important to the world than small men with great views. But given good men, such men as were produced even by the self-centred theology of an older generation, and add that wider outlook and social ideal which are coming to be the characteristics of the religion of this age, and Christianity has an equipment for the reconstruction of the world, before which nothing can stand. Such good men will not merely content themselves with being good men. They will be forces—according to their measure, public forces. They will take the city in hand, some a house, some a street, and some the whole. Of set purpose they will serve. Not ostentatiously, but silently, in ways varied as human nature, and many as life's opportunities, they will minister to its good.

To help the people, also, to be good people good fathers, and mothers, and sons, and citizens—is worth all else rolled into one. Arrange the government of the City as you may, perfect all its philanthropic machinery, make righteous its relations great and small, equip it with galleries and parks, and libraries and music, and carry out the whole programme of social reform, and the one thing needful is still without the gates. The gospel of material blessedness is part of a gospel—a great and Christian part—but when held up as the whole gospel for the people it is as hollow as the void of life whose circumference even it fails to touch.

There are countries in the world—new countries—where the people, rising to the rights of government, have already secured almost all that reformers cry for. The lot of the working man there is all but perfect. His wages are high, his leisure great, his home worthy. Yet in tens of thousands of cases the secret of life is unknown.

It is idle to talk of Christ as a social reformer if by that is meant that His first concern was to improve the organization of society, or provide the world with better laws. These were among His objects, but His first was to provide the world with better men. The one need of every cause and every community still is for better men. If every workshop held a Workman like Him who worked in the carpenter's shop at Nazareth, the labour problem and all other workman's problems would soon be solved. If every street had a home or two like Mary's home in Bethany, the domestic life of the city would be transformed in three generations.

External reforms—education, civilization, public schemes, and public charities—have each their part to play. Any experiment that can benefit by one hairbreadth any single human life is a thousand times worth trying. There is no effort in any single one of these directions but must, as Christianity advances, be pressed by Christian men to ever further and fuller issues. But those whose hands have tried the ways, and the slow work of leavening men one by one with the spirit of Jesus Christ.

The thought that the future, that any day, may see some new and mighty enterprise of redemption, some new departure in religion, which shall change everything with a breath and make all that is crooked straight, is not at all likely to be realized. There is nothing wrong with the lines on which redemption runs at present except the want of faith to believe in them, and the want of men to use them. The Kingdom of God is like leaven, and the leaven is with us now. The quantity at work in the world may increase but that is all. For nothing can ever be higher than the Spirit of Christ or more potent as a regenerating power on the lives of men.

Do not charge me with throwing away my brief because I return to this old, old plea for the individual soul. I do not forget that my plea is for the City. But I plead for good men, because good men are good leaven. If their goodness stop short of that, if the leaven does not mix with that which is unleavened, if it does not do the work of leaven—that is, to *raise something*—it is not the leaven of Christ. The question or good men to ask themselves is: Is my goodness helping others? Is it a private luxury, or is it telling upon the City? Is it bringing any single human soul nearer happiness or righteousness?

If you ask what particular scheme you shall take up, I cannot answer. Christianity has no set schemes. It makes no choice between conflicting philanthropies, decides nothing between competing churches, favours no particular public policy, organizes no one line of private charity. It is not essential even for all of us to take any public or formal line. Christianity is not all carried on by Committees, and the Kingdom of God has other ways of coming than through municipal reforms. Most of the stones for the building of the City of God, and all the best of them, are made by *mothers*. But whether or no you shall work through public channels, or only serve Christ along the quieter paths of home, no man can determine but yourself.

There is an almost awful freedom about Christ's religion. "I do not call you servants." He said, "for the servant knoweth not what his lord doeth. I have called you friends." As Christ's friends, His followers are supposed to know what He wants done, and for the same reason they will try to do it—this is the whole working basis of Christianity. Surely next to its love for the chief of sinners the most touching thing about the religion of Christ is its amazing trust in the least of saints. Here is the mightiest enterprise ever launched upon this earth, mightier even than its creation, for it is its re-creation, and the carrying of it out is left, so to speak, to haphazard—to individual loyalty, to free enthusiasms, to uncoerced activities, to an uncompelled response to the pressures of God's Spirit. Christ sets His followers no tasks. He appoints no hours. He allots no sphere. He Himself simply went about and did good. He did not stop life to do some special thing which should be called religious. His life was His religion. Each day as it came brought round in the ordinary course its natural ministry. Each village along the highway had someone waiting to be helped. His pulpit was the hillside, His congregation a woman at a well. The poor, wherever He met them, were His clients; the sick, as often as He found them, His opportunity. His work was everywhere; His workshop was the world. One's associations of Christ are all of the wayside. We never think of Him in connection with a Church We cannot picture Him in the garb of a priest or belonging to any of the classes who specialize religion. His service was of a universal human order. He was the Son of Man, the Citizen.

This, remember, was the highest life ever lived, this informal citizen-life. So simple a thing it was, so natural, so human, that those who saw it first did not know it was religion, and Christ did not pass among them as a very religious man. Nay, it is certain, and it is an infinitely significant thought, that the religious people of His time not only refused to accept this type of religion as any kind of religion at all, but repudiated and denounced Him as its bitter enemy.

Inability to discern what true religion is, is not confined to the Pharisees. Multitudes still who profess to belong to the religion of Christ, scarcely know it when they see it. The truth is, men will hold to almost anything in the name of Christianity, believe anything, do anything—except its common and obvious tasks. Great is the mystery of what has passed in this world for religion.

I SAW NO TEMPLE THERE

"I saw no Church there," said John. Nor is there any note of surprise as he marks the omission of what one half of Christendom would have considered the first essential. For beside the type of religion he had learned from Christ, the Church type— the merely Church type—is an elaborate evasion. What have the pomp and circumstance, the fashion and the form, the vestures and the postures, to do with Jesus of Nazareth? At a stage in personal development, and for a certain type of mind, such things may have a place. But when mistaken for Christianity, no matter how they aid it, or in what measure they conserve it, they defraud the souls of men, and rob humanity of its dues. It is because to large masses of people Christianity has become synonymous with a Temple service that other large masses of people decline to touch it. It is a mistake to suppose that the working classes of this country are opposed to Christianity. No man can ever be opposed to Christianity who knows what it *really* is. The working men would still follow Christ if He came among them. As a matter of fact they do follow anyone, preacher or layman, in pulpit or on platform, who is the least like Him. But what they cannot follow, and must evermore live outside of, is a worship which ends with the worshipper, a religion expressed only in ceremony, and a faith unrelated to life.

Perhaps the most dismal fact of history is the failure of the great organized bodies of ecclesiasticism to understand the simple genius of Christ's religion. Whatever the best in the Churches of all time may have thought of the life and religion of Christ, taken as a whole they have succeeded in leaving upon the mind of a large portion of the world an impression of Christianity which is the direct opposite of the reality. Down to the present hour almost whole nations in Europe live, worship, and die under the belief that Christ is an ecclesiastical Christ, religion the sum of all the Churches' observances, and faith an adhesion to the Churches' creeds. I do not apportion blame; I simply record the fact. Everything that the spiritual and temporal authority of man could do has been done—done in ignorance of the true nature of Christianity—to dislodge the religion of Christ from its natural home in the heart of Humanity. In many lands the Churches have literally stolen Christ from the people; they have made the Son of Man the Priest of an Order; they have taken Christianity from the City and imprisoned it behind altar rails; they have withdrawn it from the national life and doled it out to the few who pay to keep the unconscious deception up.

Do not do the Church, the true Church at least, the injustice to think that she does not know all this. Nowhere, not even in the fiercest secular press, is there more exposure of this danger, more indignation at its continuance, than in many of the Churches of to-day. The protest against the confusion of Christianity with the Church is the most threadbare of pulpit themes. Before the University of Oxford, from the pulpit of St. Mary's, these words were lately spoken: "If it is strange that the Church of the darker ages should have needed so bitter a lesson (the actual demolition of their churches), is it not ten times stranger still

that the Church of the days of greater enlight-
enment should be found again making the chief
part of its business the organizing of the modes
of worship; that the largest efforts which are
owned as the efforts of the Church are made for
the establishment and maintenance of worship;
that our chief controversies relate to the teaching and the ministry of a system designed pri-
marily, if not exclusively, for worship; that even
the fancies and the refinements of such a system
divide us; that the breach between things secular
and things religious grows wider instead of their
being made to blend into one; and that the vast
and fruitful spaces of the actual life of mankind lie
still so largely without the gates? The old Jerusalem was all temple. The mediaeval Church was all
temple. But the ideal of the new Jerusalem was—
no temple, but a God-inhabited society. Are we
not reversing this ideal in an age when the church
still means in so many mouths the clergy, instead
of meaning the Christian society, and when nine
men are striving to get men to go to church for
one who is striving to make men realize that they
themselves are the Church?"

Yet even with words so strong as these echo-
ing daily from Protestant pulpits the superstition
reigns in all but unbroken power. And everywhere
still men are found confounding the spectacular

services of a Church, the vicarious religion of a
priest, and the traditional belief in a creed, with
the living religion of the Son of Man.

"I saw no Temple there"—the future City will
be a City without a Church. Ponder that fact, realize the temporariness of the Church, then—go and
build one. Do not imagine, because all this has
been said, that I mean to depreciate the Church.
On the contrary, if it were mine to build a City,
a City where all life should be religious, and all
men destined to become members of the Body of
Christ, the first stone I should lay there would be
the foundation-stone of a Church Why? Because,
among other reasons, the product which the
Church on the whole best helps to develop, and in
the largest quantity, is that which is most needed
by the City.

For the present, and for a long time to come,
the manufactory of good men, the nursery of the
forces which are to redeem the City, will in the
main be found to be some more or less formal,
more or less imperfect, Christian Church. Here
and there an unchurched soul may stir the multitudes to lofty deeds; isolated men; strong enough
to preserve their souls apart from the Church, but
shortsighted enough perhaps to fail to see that
others cannot, may set high examples and stimu-
late to national reforms. But for the rank and file

of us, made of such stuff as we are made of, the steady pressures of fixed institutions, the regular diets of a common worship, and the education of public Christian teaching are too obvious safe-guards of spiritual culture to be set aside. Even Renan declares his conviction that "Beyond the family and outside the State, man has need of the Church . . . Civil society, whether it calls itself a commune, a canton, or a province, a state, or fatherland, has many duties towards the improve-ment of the individual; but what it does is neces-sarily limited. The family ought to do much more, but often it is insufficient; sometimes it is wanting altogether. The association created in the name of moral principle can alone give to every man coming into this world a bond which unites him with the past, duties as to the future, examples to follow, a heritage to receive and to transmit, and a tradition of devotion to continue." Apart altogether from the quality of its contribution to society, in the mere quantity of the work it turns out it stands alone. Even for social purposes the Church is by far the greatest Employment Bureau in the world. And the man who, seeing where it falls short, withholds on that account his witness to its usefulness, is a traitor to history and to fact.

"The Church," as the preacher whom I have already quoted, most truly adds, "is a society which tends to embrace the whole life of mankind, to bind all their relations together by a Divine sanction. As such, it blends naturally with the institutions of common life—those institutions which, because they are natural and necessary, are therefore Divine. What it aims at is not the recognition by the nation of a worshipping body, governed by the ministers of public worship, which calls itself the Church, but that the nation and all classes in it should act upon Christian principle, that laws should be made in Christ's spirit of justice, that the relations of the powers of the state should be maintained on a basis of Christian equity, that all public acts should be done in Christ's spirit, and with mutual forbearance, that the spirit of Christian charity should be spread through all ranks and orders of the people. The Church will maintain public worship as one of the greatest supports of a Christian public life; but it will always remember that the true service is a life of devotion to God and man far more than the common utterance of prayer." I have said that were it mine to build a City, the first stone I should lay there would be the foundation-stone of a Church. But if it were mine to preach the first sermon in that Church, I should choose as the text, "I saw no Church therein." I should tell the people that the great use of the Church is to help men to do without it As the old ecclesiastical term has it, Church services are "diets" of worship. They are meals. All who are hungry will take them, and, if they are wise, regularly. But no workman is paid for his meals. He is paid for the work he does in the strength of them. No Christian is paid for going to Church. He goes there for a meal, for strength from God and from his fellow-worshippers to do the work of life—which is the work of Christ. The Church is a Divine institution because it is so very human an institution. As a channel of nourishment, as a stimulus to holy deeds, as a link with all holy lives, let all men use it, and to the utmost of their opportunity. But by all that they know of Christ or care for man, let them beware of mistaking its services for Christianity. What Church services really express is the want of Christianity. And when that which is perfect in Christianity is come, all this, as the mere passing stay and scaffolding of struggling souls, must vanish away.

If the masses who never go to Church only knew that the Churches were the mute expression of a Christian's *wants* and not the self-advertisement of his sanctity, they would have more respectful words for Churches. But they have never learned this. And the result in their case of confounding religion with the Church is even more serious than in the case of the professing

Christian. When they break with the Church it means to them a break with all religion. As things are it could scarce be otherwise. With the Church in ceaseless evidence before their eyes as the acknowledged custodian of Christianity; with actual stone and lime in every street representing the place where religion dwells; with a professional class moving out and in among them, holding in their hands the souls of men, and almost the keys of Heaven—how is it possible that those who turn their backs on all this should not feel outcast from the Church's God? It is not possible. Without a murmur, yet with results to themselves most disastrous and pathetic, multitudes accept this false dividing-line and number themselves as excommunicate from all good. The masses will never return to the Church till its true relation to the City is more defined. And they can never have that most real life of theirs made religious so long as they rule themselves out of court on the ground that they have broken with ecclesiastical forms. The life of the masses is the most real of all lives. It is full of religious possibilities. Every movement of it and every moment of it might become of supreme religious value, might hold a continuous spiritual discipline, might perpetuate, and that in most natural ways, a moral influence which should pervade all Cities and all States. But they must first be taught what Christianity really is, and learn to distinguish between religion and the Church. After that, if they be taught their lesson well, they will return to honour both.

Our fathers made much of "meetness" for Heaven. By prayer and fasting, by self-examination and meditation they sought to fit themselves "for the inheritance of the saints in light." Important beyond measure in their fitting place are these exercises of the soul. But whether alone they fit men for the inheritance of the saints depends on what a saint is. If a saint is a devotee and not a citizen, if Heaven is a cathedral and not a City, then these things do fit for Heaven. But if life means action, and Heaven service; if spiritual graces are acquired for use and not for ornament, then devotional forms have a deeper function. The Puritan preachers were wont to tell their people to "practise dying." Yes; but what is dying? It is going to a City. And what is required of those who would go to a City? The practice of Citizenship—the due employment of the unselfish talents, the development of public spirit, the payment of the full tax to the great brotherhood, the subordination of personal aims to the common good. And where are these to be learned? Here; in Cities here. There is no other way to learn them. There is no Heaven to those who have not learned them.

No Church however holy, no priest however earnest, no book however sacred, can transfer to any human character the capacities of Citizenship—those capacities which in the very nature of things are *necessities* to those who would live in the kingdom of God. The only preparation which multitudes seem to make for Heaven is for its Judgment Bar. What will they do in its streets? What have they learned of Citizenship? What have they practised of love? How like are they to its Lord? To "practise dying" is to practise living. Earth is the rehearsal for Heaven. The eternal beyond is the eternal here. The street-life, the home-life, the business-life, the City-life in all the varied range of its activity, are an apprenticeship for the City of God. There is no other apprenticeship for it. To know how to serve Christ in these is to "practise dying."

To move among the people on the common street; to meet them in the market-place on equal terms; to live among them not as saint or monk, but as brother-man with brother-man; to serve God not with form or ritual, but in the free impulse of a soul; to bear the burdens of society and relieve its needs; to carry on the multitudinous activities of the City—social, commercial, political, philanthropic—in Christ's spirit and for His ends: this is the religion of the Son of Man, and the only meetness for Heaven which has much reality in it.

No; the Church with all its splendid equipment, the cloister with all its holy opportunity,
are not the final instruments for fitting men for
Heaven. The City, in many of its functions, is a
greater Church than the Church. It is amid the
whirr of its machinery and in the discipline of its
life that the souls of men are really made. How
great its opportunity is we are few of us aware. It
is such slow work getting better, the daily round
is so very common, our ideas of a heavenly life are
so unreal and mystical that even when the highest
Heaven lies all around us, when we might touch it,
and dwell in it every day we live, we almost fail to
see that it is there. The Heaven of our childhood,
the spectacular Heaven, the Heaven which is a
place, so dominates thought even in our maturer
years, that we are slow to learn the fuller truth
that Heaven is a *state*. But John, who is responsible before all other teachers for the dramatic view
of Heaven, has not failed in this very allegory to
proclaim the further lesson. Having brought all
his scenery upon the stage and pictured a material Heaven of almost unimaginable splendour, the
seer turns aside before he closes for a revelation
of a profounder kind. Within the Heavenly City
he opens the gate of an inner Heaven. It is the
spiritual Heaven—the Heaven of those who serve.
With two flashes of his pen he tells the Citizens of

God all that they will ever need or care to know as to what Heaven really means. "His servants shall serve Him; and *they shall see His Face; and His Character shall be written on their characters.*"

They shall see His Face. Where? In the City. When? In Eternity? No; to-morrow. Those who serve in any City cannot help continually seeing Christ. He is there with them. He is there before them. They cannot but meet. No gentle word is ever spoken that Christ's voice does not also speak; no meek deed is ever done that the unsummoned Vision does not there and then appear. Whoso, in whatsoever place, receiveth a little child in My name receiveth Me.

This is how men get to know God—by doing His will. And there is no other way. And this is how men become like God; how God's character becomes written upon men's characters. Acts react upon souls. Good acts make good men; just acts, just men; kind acts, kind men; divine acts, divine men. And there is no other way of becoming good, just, kind, divine. And there is no Heaven for those who have not become these. For these are Heaven.

When John's Heaven faded from his sight, and the prophet woke to the desert waste of Patmos, did he grudge to exchange the Heaven of his dream for the common tasks around him? Was he not glad to be alive, and there? And would he not straightway go to the City, to whatever struggling multitude his prison-rock held, if so be that he might prove his dream and among them see His Face? Traveller to God's last City, be glad that you are alive. Be thankful for the City at your door and for the chance to build its walls a little nearer Heaven before you go. Pray for yet a little while to redeem the wasted years. And week by week as you go forth from worship, and day by day as you awake to face this great and needy world, learn to "seek a City" there, and in the service of its neediest citizen find Heaven.

Printed in the USA
CPSIA information can be obtained
at www.ICGtesting.com
JSHW011646240624
65303JS00019B/710